FRANCIS AND HIS BROTHERS

Francis

A POPULAR

HISTORY

OF THE

FRANCISCAN

FRIARS

&

His
Brothers

(((Dominic V. Monti, O.F.M.)))

ST. ANTHONY MESSENGER PRESS
Cincinnati, Ohio

Cover and book design by Mark Sullivan
Cover image: Gozzoli, Benozzo (1420-1497)
*Stories of the Life of Saint Francis: The Dream of Innocent III and
Confirmation of the Rule by Honorius III.*
Location: S. Francesco, Montefalco, Italy
Photo Credit: Scala / Art Resource, NY

LIBRARY OF CONGRESS CATALOGING-IN-PUBLICATION DATA
Monti, Dominic, 1943-
Francis and his brothers : a popular history of the Franciscan friars / Dominic Monti.
p. cm.
Includes bibliographical references (p.   ) and index.
ISBN 978-0-86716-855-6 (pbk. : alk. paper) 1. Franciscans—History. 2. Francis, of
Assisi, Saint, 1182-1226. I. Title.
BX3606.3.M66 2008
271'.3—dc22
2008050978

ISBN: 978-0-86716-855-6

Published by St. Anthony Messenger Press
28 W. Liberty St.
Cincinnati, OH 45202
www.SAMPBooks.org

Printed in the United States of America.

Printed on acid-free paper.

09 10 11 12 5 4 3 2 1

Contents

Introduction

ight centuries ago, a dozen shabbily dressed men gained entry to the Papal Court and appeared before Pope Innocent III seeking approval of what their leader called a life according to the gospel. History has come to know him as Francis of Assisi, undoubtedly one of the most popular saints in the two-thousand-year history of the church. But although the person of Francis has continued to captivate and inspire countless Christians and non-Christians as well, the movement he initiated is less familiar. Certainly, many people have come to know contemporary Franciscans and perhaps have been touched by their ministry, but they are not aware of the long and sometimes twisted path that has brought Francis' followers from their origins to where they are today. It is the aim of this modest book to make that eight-hundred-year journey somewhat clearer.

I have been on that journey now for over forty years. I first came to know the Franciscan friars who assisted in my home parish on weekends when I was growing up. Their sermons always seemed more interesting and down-to-earth than our pastor's, and I could not help being fascinated by their habit and their sandaled feet. Then I enrolled at St. Bonaventure University and came to know them in a deeper way—as teachers, mentors and friends. And so I decided to join them. I have always been fascinated by stories from the past—especially the stories of my own family's roots and those of my adopted Franciscan family. That natural interest was sharpened by becoming educated as a historian. Then, about twenty years ago, I received the invitation to teach a survey course of Franciscan history during the summer session of the Franciscan Institute at St. Bonaventure University. I have continued doing so most summers since, and I believe that my students, most of them Franciscans, have enjoyed seeing the various threads of their history woven together to form a larger picture.

Few people, however, have the opportunity to take such a course, and so I was eager to respond to the invitation of Father Jeremy Harrington, O.F.M., then publisher of St. Anthony Messenger Press, to write a popular survey of the life and ministry of the Franciscan friars over the eight centuries of our history. Although there are a number of excellent scholarly studies in English on various aspects of that long story, there is unfortunately not a good overview readily available for people who might be interested in learning something about it. Although two books appeared about two decades ago, *A Short History of the Franciscan Family* by Damien Vorreux and Aaron Pembleton (Franciscan Herald, 1989) and William Short's fine brief introduction, *The Franciscans* (Glazier, 1989), both of these are currently out of print.

The projected length of this volume placed some parameters on both its depth and its breadth. This book is clearly not intended to be a scholarly history; such would demand a truly massive volume, and given the specialization in the various periods and cultures treated, it would have to be a team effort, not the work of one person. Secondly, I could not in such a short compass do justice to the history of the whole Franciscan movement—that is, of the three Franciscan orders: the Friars Minor, the Poor Clares and the Third Order in both its

Regular and Secular branches—without producing simply an outline of an eight-hundred-year story, rather than a narrative. So, as the title of this book implies, I have recounted only the history of the "First" Franciscan Order, the Friars Minor or Lesser Brothers in their various branches. The task of synthesizing that history into a brief volume such as this has proved challenging enough!

In one way, I was reluctant to take such a step because doing so fragments what is one great Franciscan movement. And yet each of the three Franciscan Orders does have its own unique expression of Francis' evangelical way of life in the church, and their stories have evolved in quite different ways. I hope that my book might be the first in a series—with other popular histories treating the Poor Clares, the Secular Franciscans and the Third Order Regular congregations. In fact, the story of the Third Order Regular women's congregations has already been provided in recent years by Raffaele Pazzelli and Pierre Péano.

In recounting the eight-century story of the Franciscan friars in just ten brief chapters, I have not distributed the material evenly. In fact, I have devoted three chapters to the first quarter century of the Order's history. I have done so purposely: first, to present a more accurate picture of Francis and the beginnings of his brotherhood in its historical context and second, to see how that brotherhood quickly became caught up in the pastoral needs of the thirteenth century church, thus setting a course for its future direction. Two more chapters cover the next century of the Order's growth, for as those new directions were affirmed and institutionalized, this gave rise to internal dissension among Franciscans. The other five chapters cover broader segments of the brotherhood's subsequent history, bringing it up to the present day. Since this book is written with an English-speaking audience in mind, I have tilted my narrative somewhat to focus on the history of the Order in the English-speaking world. My hope is that this work will be both interesting and informative for those seeking to learn a bit more about the Franciscan friars. If this book has accomplished that, I will be grateful.

I am most grateful to Lisa Biedenbach, editorial director of the book division of St. Anthony Messenger Press and Katie Carroll, my editor for this volume, for their support, patience and tenacity in urging me to complete this project amid my administrative responsibilities and for the careful attention they have given my work.

This year my alma mater, St. Bonaventure University, celebrates the 150th anniversary of its founding and its not insignificant role in the modern Franciscan story. I dedicate this work to all the members of the Bonaventure family—my teachers, students, colleagues, fellow alumni and, in particular, my brothers—who have accompanied me over these many years on my good journey.

Dominic V. Monti, O.F.M.

The Feast of St. Bonaventure, 2008

CHAPTER ONE

Leaving the World

Each year, some four million tourists and pilgrims converge on the small Italian town of Assisi. As they cross the Spoleto valley, they first glimpse what appears in the distance to be a medieval fantasyland perched on a commanding spur of Mount Subasio. As they draw closer and ascend the winding road up the steep hill, the massive basilica of San Francesco dominates the approach. Finally,

A view of the city of Assisi.

entering within the town walls and making their way past the tour groups jostling up the narrow streets, they encounter a place entirely given over to the marketing of its most famous son and his religious and artistic heritage. The figure of Saint Francis indeed makes present-day Assisi. But in order to understand him and the shape of the movement which he initiated—the largest religious community within the Catholic church—it is important to go back eight centuries and experience a town that was not a depopulated medieval theme park—beautifully evocative as it may be—but a thriving hub of everyday life and activity. We must understand the Assisi which produced Francis.

The Assisi that visitors see today is the product of vast economic and social forces that were transforming Europe in the central Middle Ages. For the first time since the decline of the Roman Empire, people were again clustering together in towns. This development was fueled by significant developments in agriculture which furnished a better food supply and ultimately a surplus rural population, as well as greater political stability which allowed for a rebirth of long-distance trade. No longer simply fortified places which served as military and administrative posts, towns again became an economic and cultural force. Certainly, medieval cities were modest in comparison to their modern counterparts: By 1300 there were probably only about one hundred towns in Western Europe which had over ten thousand inhabitants, and just four cities boasting more than one hundred thousand. And yet they presented a challenging environment for medieval men and women, as the contrast between town and country life was much greater than in contemporary industrialized societies. Town walls marked a real frontier between two distinct worlds.

Home for the inhabitants of a typical farming village was a tightly knit community of perhaps twenty or thirty households. The rhythms of life, defined by immemorial custom, were extremely constricting but at the same time provided a deep sense of belonging. When country people moved into a town this secure sense of the world was shattered: They may have experienced greater opportunities, but they also felt a sense of isolation. This was not simply due to the risk of anonymity in a larger setting. In the village, virtually everyone— except for the lord of the manor—was at the same subsistence level: A system of cooperative labor meant everyone rose and fell together in times of plenty or famine. In contrast, the laissez-faire dynamics of the new profit economy led to unbridled competition, pitting people against one another. To protect their mutual interests, workers in the same trade began to band together in guilds. But even so, sharp gulfs in income quickly emerged. The merchants, bankers and professionals who dominated the urban economy could amass considerable wealth, whereas the typical day laborer might work sixteen hours a day amid wretched conditions. Surviving thirteenth-century tax records clearly indicate this class polarization. The poorest people— indigents relying on alms—typically accounted for about 10 percent of the urban population. Another considerable segment, about 20 percent, owned no property, living from day to day on what they earned through their labor. The incapacitation or death of the family wage earner could quickly push families into the ranks of the beggars. These isolating tendencies were reflected on the political level. Village life was bound by the tight strictures of manorial law. City life offered enterprising peasants freedom, but they found that it often came at the price of chronic social instability.

Assisi street scene. The narrow streets would have been clogged with activity in medieval times.

Civil strife was especially endemic in northern and central Italy, where a three-sided political struggle had created a virtual power vacuum. The region was historically subject to the Holy Roman emperor, who dwelt in far-off Germany, exercising authority through his feudal vassals. But in the late eleventh century a potent new political force emerged as the popes, following the lead of Gregory VII (1073–1085), asserted the "liberty of the church" in order to free themselves from the control of powerful lay lords. Paradoxically, Gregory and his successors came to believe that the best guarantee of their spiritual freedom lay in securing their political independence. And so, medieval popes sought to establish their hegemony over a large swath of central Italy, placing themselves in conflict with the emperor. Local bishops found themselves with divided loyalties; traditionally, under imperial rule, they often had functioned in the role of chief civic authority. But as the Gregorian reform agenda took hold, the popes expected bishops to advance their claims over against imperial prerogatives. Furthermore, newly assertive commoners began to seize *de facto* power in many towns, entering mutual aid pacts to keep peace and administer justice.

Frederick I Barbarossa, Holy Roman Emperor from 1152–1190, was the feudal overlord of Assisi in Francis' youth.

Although the Emperor Frederick I Barbarossa (1152–1190) attempted to reassert his authority in the region, the stiff resistance he met from city dwellers forced him in 1183 to concede them the right to form autonomous communal governments. These quickly fell under the control of the economically dominant merchants, bankers and landowners. But as time went on, the so-called lesser guilds of artisans and shopkeepers also began agitating for a voice. Italian communes were thus inherently unstable, sharply divided by pro-imperial (Ghibelline) and pro-papal (Guelph) factions and with various classes jockeying for power. The situation was aggravated by the fact that local governmental structures were still in their infancy, providing neither comprehensive legislation nor effective administration. Families instead relied on private mutual-aid associations to protect themselves against enemies; vendettas, even civil wars, were common.

Both urban economics and politics, then, were characterized by greed and the quest for power, tending to isolate individuals from one another. To achieve anything, people found they had to join with others in organized groups such as trade guilds and mutual defense associations. But these urban communities were not a given; they had to be created by individual commitment. In this new situation which demanded personal decision making, people naturally turned to their religious faith for guidance and norms but found little to assist them. It is true that Italian communes of the period enjoyed a rich religious life in many respects. In most of them, the cathedral remained the sole baptismal church; for celebration of the Mass and other sacraments, people gathered in small communities of about forty to fifty families in their neighborhood church. However, mere ritual participation in the traditional liturgy no longer satisfied many. And people did not possess many personal religious resources—the vast majority had never received any formal instruction in their Catholic faith. This created in medieval town-dwellers an immense religious hunger. They were searching for a "word from God" to nourish them. The new social and economic realities impelled them to search for a more adequate spiritual framework.

This new situation posed severe challenges for the church. Its existing ministerial structures were ill equipped to address it. The typical priest was theologically uneducated, a situation perhaps excusable in a rural setting where his role was mainly to perform the church's rituals and transmit a few basic teachings. But since most clergymen did not enjoy permission to preach, they were in no position to offer the type of spiritual nourishment people in the towns were demanding. However, as the rising popular classes struggled to gain power from the aristocracy, they naturally viewed the institutional church as a political adversary. Both the diocesan clergy and monasteries were supported by their landed estates and the payment of obligatory tithes, setting them up as "lords" in the eyes of commoners. Ironically, the Gregorian reform—which called for a return to the ideals of the apostolic church—contributed to popular dissatisfaction by raising popular expectations of the clergy. Furthermore, an increasingly literate urban population was also dissatisfied with the purely passive role traditionally assigned them in spiritual matters. They were drawn instead to a new affective piety which emphasized the direct personal relationship of the individual to God, rather than simple cultic worship.

The Cathedral of San Rufino was the center of Assisi's religious life in Francis' time.

Confronted with the wealth and careerism of a largely inadequate clerical establishment, laypeople began to take their spiritual lives into their own hands. It was natural for townspeople who were banding together in trade guilds and mutual protection societies to form religious confraternities as well. Some of these began to reflect together on the meaning of Scripture, leading to new forms of lay piety. Attracted to the

Gospel portrayal of Jesus and his first disciples, more people came to think that a truly "apostolic life" should be poor and humble, divorced from feudal wealth and power, and engaged in evangelical preaching.

The most radical of these new movements was led by the Cathars, who revived the old dualistic heresy of the Manicheans of late antiquity. They believed that there were two distinct worlds: a spiritual one (souls) created by the good God and an intrinsically evil one (the material world) produced by Satan. The whole of Cathar religious practice was thus directed toward disengaging the soul from the corrupting influence of material things. At first glance, it would seem that this rigorist sect might have difficulty attracting followers. However, in a world marked by almost constant suffering, their message offered a plausible explanation for its pain. Furthermore, the Cathar wandering preachers, the "Perfect Ones," were credible because their ascetic way of life stood in vivid contrast to worldly Catholic clergy. By the late twelfth century, an organized Cathar anti-church was gaining adherents across Mediterranean Europe.

Given the Cathar threat, other predominantly lay movements, originally orthodox in their beliefs, soon found themselves outside the pale of the institutional church. The largest of these were the followers of Valdez, a wealthy merchant of Lyons who had abandoned all his possessions to lead a life of penance. Having commissioned a vernacular translation of the Bible, he immersed himself in the teachings of Jesus and passionately embarked on a preaching career, calling others to conversion. He and his followers, the "Poor People of Lyons," or "Waldensians," as they came to be called, intended to "live according to the pattern of the Gospel, wandering about two by two, barefooted, clad in woolen garments, holding all things in common like the apostles." They proved to be powerful opponents of the Cathars. Valdez journeyed to Rome in 1179, gaining approbation of Alexander III for his small band, but the pope also ordered them not to preach except when requested to do so by the local clergy.

However, they ignored this mandate and soon were excommunicated. In response, many Waldensians were radicalized, renouncing the authority of what they viewed as a corrupt Catholic clerical establishment. Thus, in 1184, when fearful bishops, led by Pope Lucius III, gathered at the synod of Verona with Emperor Frederick to enact legislation against the Cathars, the Waldensians were also included in their condemnations.

Assisi, the birthplace of the Franciscan movement, was a microcosm of the trends we have just examined. Situated on a major trade route through the Italian peninsula, it was ideally situated to take advantage of the expanding economy. The town's prosperity is indicated by the fact that it was forced to expand its walls twice in the space of just five decades to accommodate its burgeoning population.

For generations, Assisi had been controlled by about twenty families of the old landed aristocracy who traditionally supported the emperors in their perennial conflicts with the popes. Frederick Barbarossa had rewarded their loyalty in 1160, granting Assisi the rank of an autonomous county. But as the empire and the papacy continued to be at loggerheads in the later twelfth century, the commoners of Assisi took advantage of the unstable situation. Deserting the imperial camp in 1174, they established an independent communal government. However, the upstart city was quickly overcome; in 1177 the emperor's henchman, Conrad of Urslingen, refeudalized Assisi, ruling it from the fortress, the Rocca Maggiore, which dominated the town.

The Rocca Maggiore dominating Assisi. The present fortress is a later medieval construction.

This was the situation when Francis was born in Assisi, probably in late 1181 or early 1182, the son of Pietro di Bernardone, one of the town's wealthier merchants. According to the term used in the Assisi statutes, Pietro was a *franciarlo*, a merchant specializing in the sale of *panni franceschi*, or luxury fabrics, which he obtained at annual cloth fairs in Champagne, where merchants from all of Western Europe gathered. In fact, Francis was born while his father was away on such a journey. Although his mother had christened him John, on his father's return he named the boy Francesco, "the Frenchman," probably a word play on the source of the family's prosperity. Although later medieval legends would claim that Pietro's wife, Pica, was herself of French aristocratic descent, there actually seems little reason to doubt that she too was of local Assisi stock. In any event, Pietro was very successful in business; we know from town records that he invested a good deal of his proceeds in real estate, purchasing extensive rural properties, no doubt as a hedge against the risks of the cloth trade.

Francis was brought up by his father to eventually take over the family business. He received a basic education at the church of San Giorgio in Assisi, where the priest instructed pupils in the rudiments of reading, writing and arithmetic. Later in life, Francis would refer to himself as *simplex et idiota*—"ignorant and unlearned"—but he made this remark when comparing himself to the educated clerics who were increasingly entering his brotherhood. The very fact that Francis could read and write set him apart from the vast majority of his contemporaries. But there was no need for him to pursue studies at a university; an elementary education was more than adequate for a future merchant.

About the age of thirteen, then, Francis would have begun working with his father as a junior partner in the family business. No doubt he accompanied Pietro on trips to the Champagne fairs, in the course of which he seems to have picked up some French. This fact is important to

Memorial in Assisi to Pietro and Pica, the parents of Francis.

keep in mind. Often, we project back onto Francis our modern Western society's prolonged adolescence, at least for college-educated youth, who often do not really begin to settle down in a career or marriage until their late twenties. Francis, in contrast, had his life cut out for him early on; he plunged into a career as a merchant in which, over a decade, given a winning personality and natural communication skills, he proved quite successful. His first biographer clearly states that "he was most prudent in business," not simply a carefree adolescent. On the other hand, it is evident from the sources that Francis also enjoyed to the hilt the affluent lifestyle his parents could afford. He lavished money freely on fine clothing and partying with his companions. His family's wealth even gained him some friends among the children of the local aristocracy; indeed, Francis strove to imitate the courtly manners of the privileged classes and, if possible, gain access to their circle—perhaps through a felicitous marriage—as a knight.

But Francis' youth was not all work and play. Assisi during these years was experiencing many of the same social tensions that were convulsing other towns in Italy. Emperor Henry VI died suddenly in 1197, and with no clear successor in sight, the political situation in central Italy was thrown into chaos. The nascent communes seized the power vacuum to further their own advantage; the newly elected Pope Innocent III (1198–1216), seeking to strengthen his own hand in the region, supported these local attempts at greater autonomy. In Assisi, the commoners, scenting a whiff of freedom, revolted against the hated imperial presence. Forming a militia—of which Francis was undoubtedly a part—in 1198 they stormed the citadel that dominated the town, razing it to the ground. In its place, the citizens again organized a communal government, using the stones from the dismantled Rocca to construct a wall enclosing the city. This action unleashed pent-up class tensions within Assisi: Since the aristocratic families, based in their rural castles, still pledged loyalty to the imperial cause, the commoners vented their anger by ransacking the townhouses of the nobility. Many of the displaced knights took refuge in Assisi's bitter rival, Perugia, across the valley. Smaller towns in the area took sides in the emerging conflict, as each of the two cities made raids into the territory of the other.

The Assisi militia, in which Francis was outfitted as a knight, attempted to launch a decisive blow against Perugia in November 1202, but instead suffered a humiliating defeat. Since Francis appeared to be a man of means who could probably supply a ransom, he was taken captive and brought back to Perugia. There he languished in a dank jail for a year. Finally, toward the end of 1203, a truce was reached. Francis was released and returned home. But his long confinement had created an opportunity for him to reevaluate his direction in life. Although he returned to his former work and amusements, they no longer offered the same fulfillment. Francis did grasp at one more attempt at worldly glory, this time to battle for the church. In 1204, he joined a regiment being formed by a local Umbrian lord to join the crusade of Count Walter of Brienne, then fighting for papal interests in southern Italy. But shortly after leaving Assisi, Francis abruptly abandoned the effort and returned home.

Over the next two years, Francis began to embark upon what contemporaries referred to as a "life of penance." For Francis, this was not restricted to performing certain ascetical exercises—prayers and acts of self-denial—but achieving a whole new perspective on reality: to begin to see the world from God's point of view and to reorient the entirety of his existence in light of that perspective. Shortly before his death, in a brief document he called his *Testament*, Francis would recall the critical stages of how "the Lord led him to begin doing penance."

Francis recalls that the first step in his life of penance was when God's grace overcame his natural fear and revulsion of lepers and led him to "show mercy" to them instead. Here Francis alludes to one of the great prejudices of his epoch. For reasons that remain uncertain, in the twelfth century there seems to have been an upsurge of the incidence of leprosy in Western Europe, which in turn provoked a severe reaction by society. The grotesque appearance and revolting stench of those plagued with the disease naturally played into the ancient belief that leprosy was God's punishment for sin, which could be spread to others by the poisoned breath of its carriers. Thus, like most of his contemporaries, Francis viewed lepers not simply as unfortunates afflicted with a disfiguring disease, but as pariahs to be shunned by Christian society. The popular loathing of those afflicted by the disease led church leaders to fall back on Old Testament norms: In 1179, the Third Lateran Council ordered that lepers be segregated from other Christians into their own communities, even provided with their own churches and cemeteries. Throughout Europe, hospices for lepers were constructed on the outskirts of towns to house those afflicted with the disease. Although devout Christians provided funds for the maintenance of these facilities, they scrupulously kept a safe distance from their inmates.

Later accounts of Francis' conversion—often repeated by modern biographers—depict him as meeting an individual leper along the road, whom he embraced and gave a coin. The leper then suddenly disappeared and Francis realized that he had encountered Christ. Francis' own account of his conversion was far less dramatic but

A leper with his bell (from a fourteenth-century manuscript).

much more demanding: Although he may well have met a leper along the road, the important thing is that this encounter spurred a change in his outlook. Francis overcame his natural fear and revulsion to actually go out to the leper communities at San Rufino dell'Arce and San Lazaro in the valley below Assisi, where he would stay among these marginal-ized people to serve their needs. It is important to recognize here that the beginnings of Francis' conversion were not specifically religious in nature. Rather, it involved a conversion from a social order based on self-protection and self-aggrandizement to one based on mutual affirmation and self-sacrifice.

Francis' emerging view of other people was coupled with a new perspective on God. He found himself being tugged away from his daily routine to seek God's voice. In a particular way, his *Testament* recalls that he was drawn to deserted country chapels where he prayed for God's guidance. Francis felt himself especially attracted to the small, tumble-down church of San Damiano, on the side of a steep hill below Assisi, where the powerful image on the crucifix there led him to grasp the paradoxical manifestation of God's love in the world. As he tells us, "I would pray with simplicity and say: 'We adore you, Lord Jesus Christ, in all your churches throughout the whole world, and we bless you because by your holy cross you have redeemed the world.'" He came to realize that it was precisely by Christ's decision to empty himself totally that the abundance of God's life had entered the world. He began to recognize that God's logic, manifest in the Incar-nation and on Calvary, was the reverse of the standards that prevailed in Assisi. Christ had revealed a different way of living, completely con-trary to the quest for security, wealth and power. More and more, Francis came to realize that Christ's embrace of human poverty, his acceptance of human suffering and death in obedience to his Father's will, were not simply past

The Church of San Damiano.

actions that had redeemed human beings from the power of sin, but meant "to leave us an example, that we might follow in his footsteps." He increasingly recognized that he must follow that path of self-emptying.

His growing awareness of God's ways soon precipitated a total break with the ways of Assisi. One of the early biographies of Francis recounts that one day, most likely in the year 1206, he was praying in the church of San Damiano when he suddenly felt that the image of Christ on the cross was speaking to him directly: "Francis," it said, "go rebuild my house; as you see, it is all being destroyed." Still impelled by dramatic images of chivalrous behavior, Francis decided he must rebuild the house of God in which he experienced God's grace. He knew immediately where he would find the money to do so. He hurried home, took several bolts of expensive cloth from the family shop and rode to the nearby town of Foligno where he sold both the cloth and his horse; then, he returned back to San Damiano where he gave the coins to the priest there. Naturally, Francis' father was enraged by his actions. In fear, Francis hid from his father for some time but eventually emerged to beg for more supplies for the church. Word reached his father, who stormed down to San Damiano to call his son to his senses. Failing in this, he took his case to the communal government, filing a claim against Francis and demanding restitution. The consuls recog-

An interior view of San Damiano with a copy of the cross venerated by Francis. (The original crucifix is presently in the basilica of St. Clare in Assisi.)

nized that Francis' evident determination to become a public penitent placed him under the authority of the church rather than civil
court and thus referred the case to the newly elected bishop, Guido.
When both Francis and his father appeared before him, Guido told
Francis that if he wished to work on behalf of the church, he had to
return to his father all that remained of his money. Francis
responded in a dramatic gesture: He stripped himself naked, hand-
ing over his clothing with the coins piled on top. The stunned
observers heard these words: "Until now, I have called Pietro
Bernardone my father. But because I have proposed to serve God, I
return the money and the clothing that is his. From now on, I want
to say, not 'my father Pietro Bernardone,' but 'our Father, who is in
heaven.' " Francis had uttered his farewell to the world.

*An image of Francis renouncing his belongings, from
the upper basilica of San Francesco, Assisi.*

The Lord Gave Me Brothers

rancis' dramatic decision to break with his father and "leave the world" meant that he had become a kind of leper himself, forced to fashion a new existence on the margins of Assisi society. For the first year or two, he spent much of his time alone, devoting himself to prayer and repairing several small chapels in the rural areas around Assisi while continuing to minister among the lepers. From the church's perspective, Francis was a lay penitent hermit, one of many such freelance religious who were a prominent feature of life in central Italy. As such, he enjoyed the protection of Bishop Guido. It is ironic that this prelate, known to be an avaricious, litigious man intent on maintaining his rights and privileges, remained a faithful supporter and spiritual guide of Francis, who was so committed to reconciliation and peace.

But Francis' journey of "doing penance" was only just beginning. About two years later, in 1208, his life took a further turn, as he recalled in his *Testament*, "when the Lord gave me brothers" and "revealed to me that I should live according to the form of the Holy Gospel." One day, two other citizens of Assisi, Bernard of Quintavalle, like Francis from an upper-middle class family, and another man, known only as Peter, approached him, wishing to share his life. According to one early account, Francis suggested they seek direction from God, and so the three went up to Assisi, entered the Church of St. Nicholas on the town square and asked the priest if they might see the Gospel of Christ. The priest presented them with a missal; then Francis, following a popular religious practice for discerning God's will, paused to pray and then opened the book three times at random. Each time, their eyes fell on a Gospel passage that spoke of the radical renunciation to which Jesus called his followers: his invitation to the rich young man to sell everything he possessed and give the money to the poor (Mark 10:21), his demand that they deny themselves and take up their cross (Matthew 16:24), and his

instructions to the apostles to take nothing for the journey as they went out to proclaim God's reign (Luke 9:3). Francis saw these texts as confirming his own decision to renounce his belongings and social status and indicating to his new companions the path they also must take if they were to follow the self-emptying path marked out by Jesus. And so Bernard and Peter also abandoned everything they owned and came to live with Francis. Within a few days, a young peasant named Giles, also joined their ranks. They settled at one of the little churches that Francis had rebuilt, St. Mary of the

The Church of St. Mary of the Angels (the Portiuncula) in Assisi. In the sixteenth century, a massive basilica was built over the little chapel that Francis restored—the birthplace of his brotherhood.

Angels, several miles from Assisi down in the valley, not far from one of the leper hospices. This property, called the Portiuncula or "Little Portion," belonged to the local Benedictine abbey on Mt. Subasio; the abbot allowed Francis and his brothers to stay on this virtually worthless piece of land, where they constructed a small hut near the church. Over the next months, eight others joined the new movement, including a local knight, Angelo Tancredi.

Francis and his first companions settled at the Portiuncula precisely because they believed their gospel way of life demanded that they maintain the social location of hermits. Thus it was that they chose to dwell physically apart from "the world," in a remote, abandoned place on the edge of settled Assisi—on property which legally belonged to others. There the brothers remained outsiders to the city, living—as their Rule would later express it—"among people of little worth and looked down upon, among the poor and powerless, the sick and the lepers, and the beggars by the wayside." It was from the perspective of these other marginalized people that they viewed the urban life of Assisi. During these years, the aristocratic and popular parties—dominated by the well-to-do merchants and professional classes—within the commune of Assisi were settling their differences, finally entering a "Great Pact" in 1210 to assure the peace and prosperity of the city. Although a communal government was again established, it was controlled by the wealthy commoners, as only they could afford the payment required for exemption from feudal levies and the right to participate as full voting citizens. Francis and his companions recognized that this compact still disenfranchised the large majority of Assisi's population. In contrast, they had chosen to "leave the world" in the way they did because they had come to see that the values of the reign of God were in sharp contrast to the values that dominated life in the commune. Instead of accepting the society driven by the quest for power and wealth in which they had been born and bred, the brothers deliberately chose "to follow the humility and poverty of our Lord, Jesus Christ." This was the only way they felt they could escape the vicious circle in which their contemporaries were caught and which prevented them from opening their hearts to God and each other.

And yet Francis also believed that this new gospel life involved a mission to that same world. He and his brothers did not spend all their time at the Portiuncula in the manner of traditional hermits; rather, following the example of Jesus and his apostles, they also chose to interact on a regular basis with the other people of Assisi. Franciscan scholar David Flood has expressed this paradox well: "They had left the world to get closer to people," changing the way they lived in it, laboring at the same jobs as other people, but using the good things of God's creation in such a way as not to deprive others of them. Although they dwelt down in the valley some distance from Assisi, they would trek back up into the city or to the leper hospices to work. There they practiced the trades they knew, but no longer for profit. Refusing to accept money as wages, they received only the necessities of life—food, clothing and shelter—which they shared among themselves and with the poor. In this way, with no property to defend and no agenda of material gain, they were free to approach all people as equal in God's sight, worthy of attention and concern.

It was out of this paradoxical situation, working in the midst of a world whose values they rejected, that the early brothers began to preach a message of penance to others: "Do penance, performing worthy fruits of penance because we shall soon die. Give and it will be given to you....Forgive and you shall be forgiven." The brothers urged those who had more than they did to free themselves from worldly concerns, to live simply and to demonstrate the sincerity of their love for God by reconciling themselves to their enemies and by reaching out to help their less fortunate neighbors. Through the example of their own converted life and their preaching they could assist their sisters and brothers who remained in the city to reject its demons of violence and greed.

Their desire to spread this message impelled Francis in the fall of 1208 to split up the brothers; they traveled in pairs throughout the region as heralds of God's reign, inviting people to reform their lives. It was probably this decision to move beyond the immediate confines of Assisi that caused Francis to realize that they needed greater authorization than Bishop Guido's. And so, in 1209, he had the basic elements of his new gospel way of life written down in a brief document, and the twelve brothers journeyed to Rome to seek the approval of Pope Innocent III. Fortunately for them, Innocent was significantly more liberal than his immediate predecessors in granting church recognition to popular evangelical movements—including several groups formerly branded heretical. Only the year before, Innocent had reconciled a group of former Waldensians who wished to continue their vocation as popular Gospel preachers within the boundaries of the Catholic church. The two things Innocent demanded of such groups were unswerving allegiance to Catholic doctrine and obedience to the church's hierarchy. Although later accounts of his meeting with Francis indicate the pope's hesitancy in approving yet another potentially troublesome grassroots movement, Innocent was sufficiently convinced by Francis' orthodoxy and respect for authority to grant in

A depiction of the approval of Francis' gospel way of life by Pope Innocent III, from the upper basilica of San Francesco, Assisi.

consistory formal, if only oral, approval of the new brotherhood. He also gave Francis permission to preach penance publicly, as well as to any other brothers Francis so allowed. One of the pope's advisors suggested giving the brothers a small tonsure as a badge of their ecclesiastical approval.

Returning to Assisi, the brothers decided at first to settle in what was no more than a shed in a place called Rivo Torto, about two miles up the valley from the Portiuncula, not far from a leper hospice. But when a local farmer decided to reclaim the property, they returned to St. Mary of the Angels. This would remain the home base of the rapidly growing brotherhood for the rest of Francis' life. It was about this time that the group, who had hitherto been known simply as "penitents from Assisi" decided to call themselves *fratres minores*, "Lesser Brothers." This term captured two of the basic features of their life: their determination to remain truly "minors" or "lesser ones" in society, without power and possessions, and to create among themselves a new type of relationship. The common English name for the brotherhood, "Friars Minor," is a very literal translation of the Latin title ('friar' being a derivative of the French *frère* ("brother").

Giotto's fresco of Clare of Assisi, from the Church of Santa Croce, Florence.

One of men who joined the brotherhood soon after their return from Rome was a young knight of Assisi named Rufino, whose extended family lived in one of the great townhouses of the feudal nobility overlooking the cathedral square. He soon told Francis about his cousin, a spirited young woman named Clare. Born about a dozen years after Francis, she and her family had been exiled from Assisi during the popular uprising in 1199, returning only at a provisional peace in 1205. Over the next several years, Clare had gradually decided to adopt the life of a penitent in the family home; committing herself to celibacy in order to devote her time to prayer, fasting and works of charity. When Francis learned of her dedicated way of life, he was determined to meet her. As a result of their conversations, Clare decided that she too was called to do penance, not simply through the devout practices she had adopted, but by following Francis' example by renouncing her property and social status. Thus it was on Palm Sunday night, 1212, Clare somehow managed to leave her family home and the walled town undetected; hastening down to the Portiuncula, she exchanged her fine garments for the rough woolen gown of a penitent.

After temporary stays with other communities of religious women, Francis arranged with Bishop Guido for Clare and several other aristocratic women who had joined her to settle at the church of San Damiano. There the "Poor Ladies" devoted themselves to prayer, supporting themselves by the work of their hands. It has traditionally been the opinion that Clare and her sisters were strictly contemplative from the start, but modern scholarship has come to support the idea that there was also a hospice at San Damiano where the sisters nursed the sick. A small community of brothers settled nearby, making San Damiano in effect a "double monastery."

One of the first eyewitnesses of this early Minorite movement was a reform-minded cleric from northern Europe, Jacques de Vitry, who visited the papal court, then residing in Perugia, in 1216:

> In this region, many well-to-do secular people have left all things for Christ and fled the world. They are called "Lesser Brothers" and "Lesser Sisters." They are held in great reverence by the Lord Pope and the Cardinals. They are in no way occupied with temporal things, but with fervent desire and ardent zeal they labor each day to draw from the vanities of the world souls that are perishing, and draw them to their way of life.... During the day the brothers

go into the cities and villages giving themselves over to the active life in order to gain others; at night, however, they return to their hermitage or solitary places to devote themselves to contemplation. The women dwell together near the cities in various hospices, accepting nothing, but living by the work of their hands.... With great profit, the brothers of this Order assemble once a year in a designated place to rejoice in the Lord and eat together; with the advice of good men they draw up and promulgate holy laws and have them confirmed by the Lord Pope. After this they disperse again for the whole year throughout Lombardy and Tuscany, Apulia and Sicily.

Several things are evident in Jacques's description. First of all, he captures the novelty of the early Franciscan movement: men and women who had abandoned their possessions, voluntarily living among the lesser ones of society, creating a new fraternity of care and compassion. The sharp social distinctions that characterized contemporary society did not exist among them: The brothers and sisters accepted all comers regardless of their rank or income. Although the women led a more traditional type of life residing in hospices, the brothers clearly had an itinerant existence. This was a clear break with established patterns of religious life that presupposed a stable community. Although the brothers did tend to occupy certain places like the Portiuncula on a more or less permanent basis—in the sense that a visitor might expect to find at least some brothers there—they were constantly coming and going. Many were on the road in small groups for weeks at a time, seeking lodging wherever they could find it, while others stayed in leper hospices for shorter periods as they cared for their needs. It was up to each brother to find employment, working at the trade he knew; if the brothers could not find work, they could beg as other poor people. The brothers maintained a strong eremitical component to their life, often spending extended periods of time in their out-of-the-way retreats to devote themselves to rest and prayer. As far as participating in the church's liturgical life, they attended services in parish churches with other Catholics.

Jacques' account also reveals the support the new movement had at least among some prelates of the church. Perhaps Francis even attended the Fourth Lateran Council, called together by Innocent III in 1215. This assembly passed a wide range of reform statutes which would have a profound effect on the new Franciscan movement. One of the council's decrees in particular was intended to regularize the situation of the many new groups who were attempting to lead a more radical form of Christian life by requiring them to adopt one of the rules—either Benedict's or Augustine's—that had traditionally governed religious life in the Western Church. The new Minorite movement clearly did not fit into these existing patterns and its rapid growth gave rise to a good deal of skepticism, if not outright hostility, among many bishops as well as members of the established orders. When the brothers rendezvoused each year to hold a plenary assembly or chapter, they discussed how they were living out their commitment "to follow the teaching and footprints" of Christ and made necessary modifications to their form of life in light of challenging situations they were experiencing. It would appear from Jacques' testimony that even at this point, sympathetic advisors from the papal curia were making themselves available at these chapters to insure that the brothers' decisions were in conformity with church law.

Jacques also mentions that by 1216, the brothers, by now rapidly growing in number, were going out on missions throughout all of Italy. He also alludes to the fact that many people were responding to the brothers' call to convert their lives. Although some of these men and women chose to enter the Lesser Brothers or Poor Sisters, others, bound in marriage or other commitments to work or family, or simply not desiring to renounce totally their life in the world, determined to "do penance" on their own or by forming small penitential confraternities for mutual support. Although they had no juridical connection to the Lesser Brothers, Francis considered these

• • •

FOURTH LATERAN COUNCIL 1215

The Basilica of St. John Lateran, Rome. Principal church and residence of medieval popes, it was the scene of the great reforming Council of 1215.

Summoned by Pope Innocent III in November 1215, this was the largest of all medieval councils, attended by over 70 archbishops, 400 bishops and 900 abbots and priors of religious communities. It issued a wide range of decrees strengthening the identity of Catholic Christendom: calling for a new crusade, demanding that Jews and Muslims wear special dress and instituting measures against heresy. Among these were a profession of faith stating that there was no salvation outside the church, a ban against unauthorized preaching, and the institution of the legal process later known as the Inquisition. The council also attempted to curtail abuses among the clergy (concubinage, drunkenness, simony) and called them to give greater reverence to the Eucharist. It required bishops to ensure that adequate preaching was provided for their people. It also established a minimum requirement for Catholic Church membership by instituting the "Easter duty" of an annual confession of sins and reception of the Eucharist.

"Brothers and Sisters of Penance" his companions in leading a gospel life and would later write exhortations to them.

The following year, the annual chapter made the momentous decision to send out expeditions over the Alps and beyond the seas—to the Crusader States in the eastern Mediterranean—as well. A consequence of this decision was the need to divide the brotherhood into more manageable regional units or "provinces," with a minister designated to be in charge of each. Within Italy, six provinces were established, and five others for the new territories: Spain, Provence, (northern) France, Germany and Syria. Francis himself intended to lead the band going to France, but one of the influential churchmen who backed the new movement, Cardinal Ugolino di Segni, the plenipotentiary papal legate for central and northern Italy, convinced him to remain in Umbria, where he could be in closer contact with the majority of friars and with the Roman curia.

These first expeditions to northern Europe were largely unsuccessful. The brothers were moving into territories with a very different culture than central Italy; ignorant of local customs and unknown to the local hierarchy, they were all too easily identified with unorthodox religious groups and experienced a good deal of hostility. Within the year, many of the brothers straggled home disappointed and frustrated.

Despite these setbacks, the chapter of 1219 launched new expeditions. This time, however, a prominent curial sympathizer, probably Cardinal Ugolino, obtained from Pope Honorius III (1216–1227) a letter of introduction to be sent on ahead of them. It requested all prelates of the church to receive the Lesser Brothers as men who "have chosen a way of life deservedly approved by the apostolic see...and who go about sowing the seed of the Word of God."

Francis himself was determined to accompany one of these missions—that to the land of the "infidels." His first biographer, Thomas of Celano, recounts that Francis had for a number of years wanted to go among the Muslims to give witness to his faith. It is certainly clear from his own writings that he deeply desired that "all peoples, races, tribes and tongues, all nations and all peoples everywhere on earth" should come to know and serve the one Lord God. This included the followers of Islam, who had been demonized as enemies of the faith since the beginning of the Crusading movement in the late eleventh century. According to Thomas, Francis set off to preach to the Muslims in 1212, perhaps swept up in the popular enthusiasm of the so-called "Children's Crusade" of that year. This vast popular movement was actually composed of masses of indigent young peasants who believed that the ultimate goal of the Crusades—the liberation of Jerusalem—would be accomplished only through the conversion of the Muslims. They were convinced that their peaceful mission would succeed in contrast to the failed efforts of powerful lords who relied on their weapons of war. But Francis' attempt, like the Children's Crusade itself, was a failure; he only managed to get to the coast of Dalmatia. A few years later, he again tried to reach Muslim lands through Spain, but this time was turned back by illness.

The year 1219 would prove different. Leaving two brothers behind as his vicars to manage affairs, Francis set out for the East. A new crusade—subsequently labeled the Fifth Crusade by historians —was then underway. Innocent III had pushed the appeal to liberate the Holy Land to the forefront of the church's agenda at the Fourth Lateran Council, calling all Christians to give it their active moral support. Perhaps only some could fight, but many more could give alms, and everyone could take part in mandatory public intercessory processions for its success. After intensive efforts on the part of the papacy, the crusade itself finally got underway in 1218. It is interesting that this vast effort is not at all reflected in Francis' writings, unlike many of the other reform initiatives of the council which he strongly supported. The Lesser Brothers apparently believed they could advance the cause of Christianity, not by fighting Muslims with weapons, but through the testimony of their lives and words, even though they were fully aware that any attempt to proselytize in a Muslim nation would probably spell death.

Expeditions of brothers set out in several directions. One, led by a brother Berard, traveled through the Iberian peninsula; they received permission from the King of Castile to cross the frontier into the territory of the Almohad emirate—Al Andalus. Employing a tactic of Spanish "suicide preachers," they deliberately provoked martyrdom by entering a mosque in Seville at the hour of prayer to proclaim the truth of Christianity. Banished from there, they continued on to Morocco, where they were finally executed because they persisted in denouncing Islam. Brother Giles, the early companion of Francis, was in charge of a second expedition that had been dispatched to Tunis. There, however, local Christian merchants, fearing a hostile reaction from the Muslim population, forced them to leave. Francis and his group reached Acre, the seat of the Crusader kingdom on the coast of Palestine, but they quickly departed to join the main body of the army, which was besieging the stronghold of Damietta in the Nile delta. During a lull in the fighting, Francis and one companion succeeded crossing the enemy lines and managed to meet the sultan, Malik al-Kamil (1218–1238). They encountered not the "fierce beast" of crusading propaganda, but a man open to dialogue who was impressed by their genuine concern for his spiritual welfare.

Francis returned, not having obtained the Sultan's conversion, but rather experiencing a conversion of his own. He became even more convinced that there was another way to go among the

Francis with the Sultan.

Muslims—not by preaching the gospel in words, but by simply living out its demands among them, subject to all. Francis went from there to visit the Holy Land, but his stay in the Middle East was cut short by reports that all was not well at home with his brotherhood. He had to return.

CHAPTER THREE

Two Saints

rancis returned from the Near East to find his brotherhood in turmoil. The vicars he had left in charge during his absence had been introducing changes which were upsetting some of the brothers. The innovations they proposed aimed at bringing the Lesser Brothers more in line with practices of the established religious orders. Francis saw that the entire shape of his brotherhood was at stake, but he also recognized that the situation demanded greater organizational skills than he possessed. He immediately went to Pope Honorius III (1216–1227) and requested that he officially appoint Cardinal Ugolino "protector" of the brotherhood to defend it from outside critics and to help it surmount its evident growing pains. Furthermore, at a regional chapter that fall, Francis abdicated his day-to-day leadership role, choosing a well-educated jurist, Peter Cantanii, as general minister. Unfortunately, Peter died at the Portiuncula only six months after taking office. As his successor, Francis selected Elias, the brother who had led the first contingent of friars to the Crusader States in 1217, who had been a successful teacher and notary prior to his entry into the brotherhood. During his time in the East, Francis had been deeply impressed by Elias' abilities and brought him back to Italy with him.

The tensions facing the brotherhood were the inevitable result of its explosive numerical growth and far-flung geographical expansion, which thrust it into the attention of church leaders. Some of them were highly critical of the Lesser Brothers, clearly uncomfortable with their unconventional way of life that broke so completely with traditional patterns; a few were even demanding that the brothers be suppressed. But at the same time, others in the hierarchy were coming to recognize in the Minorites' obvious popular appeal a potential instrument to advance the church's agenda of pastoral reform. At the Fourth Lateran Council, the bishops had belatedly recognized that the great success of heretical movements was largely the result of the church's failure to address popular religious needs. Strenuous efforts would have to be made to provide a better educated clergy who could lead the laity to a reasonable understanding of the essentials of Christian belief and practice. The chief means to accomplish this goal—aimed at a largely illiterate population—would be through doctrinal preaching and one-to-one pastoral guidance in the sacrament of confession. And so Canon 10 of the council ordered bishops to appoint "suitable men to carry out...the duty of sacred preaching,...building up the people through word and example," who could also serve as "coadjutors...in hearing confessions and enjoining penances and other matters conducive to the salvation of souls." Recognizing that both of these emphases would demand that the clergy receive a more thorough theological education than had been the practice, Canon 11 prescribed the appointment of lectors "to teach Scripture to priests and others, and especially to instruct them in matters which are recognized as pertaining to the cure of souls."

The council's vision of a reformed and educated clergy did not originally involve the brotherhood of Francis of Assisi. Unlike the Order of Preachers founded by the Spaniard, Dominic of Calaruega (1170–1221), a zealous priest seeking to respond to the pastoral needs enunciated by the council, Francis' movement had risen "from below." His Lesser Brothers were largely laymen motivated primarily by their desire to renounce the "world"—the web of avarice and status-seeking they perceived as the dominant forces in their society —to create a new type of community based on authentic gospel values. They viewed their mission in the church as calling other Christians to true conversion of heart through their informal penitential preaching, but more importantly, through the witness of their own converted lives as they moved, propertyless and powerless, among their neighbors. They did not view themselves as exercising an official ministry on behalf of the church.

But that quickly changed, as Francis' brotherhood was dramatically transformed from within. Within a decade of its founding, more and more zealous young clerics were attracted to the Minorite movement. Even in the early days, we know that a few priests from Assisi had entered the brotherhood, such as Sylvester and Leo, the latter becoming prominent in later years thanks to his role as Francis' confessor and intimate companion. But many others soon followed: Jacques de Vitry's letter of 1216 mentioned that even one of the pope's closest advisors wished to join. This was because the Minorites provided an attractive option for priests who desired to "leave the world" by rejecting the careerism and corruption so dominant in the ranks

Saint Dominic, founder of the Order of Preachers, as depicted in a fourteenth-century painting of a dispute with Cathar heretics. As pastoral agents of reform in the church, Dominic's friars were friendly rivals of the Lesser Brothers in the thirteenth century.

of the clergy but who at the same time were reluctant to enter a traditional monastery because that would mean relinquishing an active
ministry. More and more young clerics saw in the Lesser Brothers an
opportunity to achieve both goals: a way to live out radical gospel values and a base from which to exercise a fruitful apostolic ministry.
Their viewpoint dovetailed with that of those prelates who wished to
enlist the Minorites in the church's pastoral mission.

Among those church leaders who were attracted to Francis' new
evangelical movement was Pope Honorius III himself. He was convinced that the urgent task of reform within the church took priority
over existing ecclesiastical structures. Although the Lateran IV
decrees had clearly intended that its pastoral program would be
dependent on local bishops, Honorius was not willing to wait for
unreformed prelates to take the initiative to implement it. His confidence that Dominic's new Order of Preachers could supply the "suitable men" called for by the council led him to foster their ministry,
largely exempting them from episcopal control. Cardinal Ugolino,
who had come to know Francis and his movement in Central Italy,
brought the Lesser Brothers to Honorius' attention, and the pope
began showering favors on them as well. Beginning in 1219 Honorius
issued a series of directives commending the new fraternity; in a clear
break from the intent of the Lateran decree against new religious
orders, he informed hesitant bishops that he considered the Lesser
Brothers to be "among those Orders approved by us." But Honorius
also began to stress the benefits the Minors offered the church
through their preaching ministry—a role that by its very nature
emphasized the role of the clerical friars.

In addition, Ugolino, precisely because he was supportive of the
Minors, wished to correct what he saw as deficiencies in the highly
unorganized brotherhood. For example, Francis was known for
accepting all comers; there was no process of formation which could
test those men who may have made a hasty decision to enter this

demanding gospel life. The spontaneity of movement that characterized the life of the early brothers also came at the price of undisci-
plined friars roaming about, causing scandal rather than edification.
If the Lesser Brothers were to gain recognition as a true religious
order, Ugolino recognized that more internal structures would be
necessary. Thus in September, 1220, Honorius issued a decree
demanding that the Minorites establish a year of novitiate or proba-
tion before a brother professed obedience to the rule, as well as making all brothers clearly responsible to their superiors, forbidding them
to "wander about outside obedience."

One of the more outstanding of the new recruits came from far-
off Portugal. Known to later history as Anthony of Padua, Fernando
Martins was born in the early 1190s in Lisbon, a city on the frontiers
between Christian and Muslim cultures. His father probably
belonged to a family of knights from northern Europe who had come
to fight in the *Reconquista*—the crusade to reclaim the Iberian
peninsula from Muslim rule—and had been rewarded with property
when Lisbon was "liberated" in 1147. There Fernando was educated
at the cathedral school, apparently destined by his parents for an
ecclesiastical career, perhaps the prestigious post of a canon of the
cathedral. However, the young Fernando disappointed their hopes by
entering a rather austere community of Augustinian canons outside
Lisbon. Distracted by the frequent visits of his family and friends, he
asked in 1212 to be transferred to the motherhouse of the congregation, the abbey of Santa Cruz in Coimbra, then the capital of the
young kingdom of Portugal. Santa Cruz was the most famous center
of religious culture in the country; with a well-stocked library and
teachers who had been educated at the great abbey of St. Victor in
Paris, it provided excellent resources for the bright young cleric.

During Anthony's years in Coimbra, some Lesser Brothers
arrived in Portugal. Through the generosity of Queen Urraca, they
settled at a small hermitage outside Coimbra dedicated to Saint

Anthony of Egypt. There they followed the practice common among the early brothers, alternating their activity between praying in the hermitage and working among people. Both the idealism and evangelistic thrust of the new brotherhood appealed to Fernando, who led a virtually cloistered existence in a highly politicized abbey. His attraction reached a climax when the bodies of Berard and his companions, the five Lesser Brothers who had been executed in Morocco in 1220, were ransomed by King Alfonso and buried as martyrs in the abbey of Santa Cruz. Fernando, fired with a desire to preach the gospel even in the face of death, received permission from his superiors to transfer to the Lesser Brothers, taking the name of the hermitage's patron, Anthony, as his own.

Almost immediately upon entering the brotherhood, Anthony sought permission from the local minister for permission to go to Africa to preach the gospel among the Muslims. Although his first biographers stress his desire for martyrdom, at least one modern historian has suggested that Anthony, who had grown up in an intercultural city where the Muslim community was very much a living presence, felt that he had a better chance of actually converting Moors rather than antagonizing them, as did the zealous but naive brothers who had been killed in their preaching attempt. However, Anthony fell sick soon after he arrived in Morocco, and then the ship bringing him back was driven off course and landed in Sicily. There Anthony searched out the local friars; in the spring of 1221 he trekked up to Assisi with them for the annual Pentecost chapter, when according to custom, all the brothers who could do so were supposed to assemble.

This was probably the great "Chapter of Mats" described by later chroniclers, when perhaps three thousand brothers converged on the Portiuncula, constructing rude shelters made from reeds. Cardinal Ranieri Capocci, a Cistercian monk, and a number of other prelates were in attendance. Brother Elias presided, but Francis tugged at the sleeve of his habit whenever he wished to make a point. The major point of discussion was the very foundation of the brotherhood's way of life. Francis had been busy since his return from the East, attempting to compile in one document his "life according to the gospel" as it had evolved over the past dozen years in light of the experience of the brothers and new church directives. He had asked Caesar of Speyer, a well-educated German priest who had probably joined the Order in the East, to assist him in this task by enriching the text with appropriate biblical passages. Francis presented this draft of the Rule to the chapter for ratification; it was then sent on to the papal court for confirmation.

Perhaps because of Brother Elias' practical approach, the missionary efforts of this chapter were organized in a much more systematic fashion. Francis very much wanted to send a new expedition to Germany in place of the one that had failed several years previously; this time, Caesar of Speyer, was designated as minister. Caesar was allowed to select whichever brothers he considered most suitable from among the many who had volunteered. The group he assembled comprised some twelve clerics and thirteen lay friars, a striking expression of the growing emphasis on the brothers' preaching ministry. The text of the Rule of 1221 also clearly indicates that a special group among the brothers was now occupied with the task of formal preaching.

One of these was Anthony, who was assigned at the same chapter to the Lombard province, which then comprised all of northern Italy. Heretical sects were much more deeply entrenched in that region than in Umbria, so the Minorites often found themselves being asked to distinguish their own message from that of the Cathars and Waldensians. In this setting, Anthony's extensive theological training quickly gained him attention, and he soon embarked on an extensive preaching campaign. Before long, he was being urged to instruct other friars in theology so they too would be equipped to explain the Catholic faith. For the Lesser Brothers, such would be a dramatic new move into uncharted waters. Just a few years previously, Francis had learned that the friars in Bologna—hoping to recruit bright young university students as the Dominicans were doing—had accepted a commodious stone house outside the city as a dwelling. In response, Francis had ordered the brothers to vacate the place, reversing his decision only when Cardinal Ugolino intervened, stating that the house belonged to him. In light of Francis' feelings, Anthony wanted to make sure he had his support to embark on this new venture. Early in 1224, Francis consented to his request: "It pleases me that you should teach sacred theology to the brothers as long as—in the words of the rule—you 'do not extinguish the spirit of

Francis preaching before Pope Honorius III.

prayer and devotion with study of this kind.'" Perhaps one might detect a note of resignation in Francis' words—on the one hand, he knew the brothers needed to make provision for a rapidly changing situation; on the other he rightly feared that the fostering of study could damage the relationship of the brothers to one another and their commitment to be poor, lesser ones among God's people. Like power and possessions, knowledge was definitely a temptation to pride and a source of inequality. Furthermore, serious study required expensive books and more established residences.

There is no doubt that during these years Francis was experiencing a certain estrangement from the accelerating developments that were quickly transforming the brothers' primitive pattern of life. Some of the early sources even refer to a "great temptation" he was experiencing at this time—namely, to give up on his own Order. The Roman curia had rejected the draft of his Rule submitted after the 1221 chapter. He therefore devoted his efforts to composing another, arriving with the help of canonists at a succinct statement of the brotherhood's basic principles. This version of the Rule finally gained official confirmation by Honorius III on November 29, 1223, thereby giving his brotherhood definitive legal existence as a religious order in the church.

THE SECOND AND THIRD FRANCISCAN ORDERS

During the 1220s, as the Lesser Brothers took the shape of an officially recognized religious order, other women and men who had been inspired by Francis' life of gospel penance also received more structured forms of life from church authority.

In the wake of the Fourth Lateran Council, Cardinal Ugolino was active in organizing a number of women's communities in central Italy. In line with prevailing contemporary ideas that religious women should be

- *sequestered from the world, he drew up a form of life in*
- *1219 for these "Poor Cloistered Nuns." After Francis'*
- *death, now Pope Gregory IX, he urged Clare and her sis-*
- *ters at San Damiano to adapt his rule rather than the*
- *brief form of life which Francis had given them. In 1228,*
- *Clare acceded to his request, although she succeeded in*
- *receiving from him a "privilege of poverty" which pro-*
- *tected her desire to maintain her ideals. In 1253, Clare*
- *finally succeeded in gaining approval for her own rule,*
- *although most of the other communities continued to fol-*
- *low the rule written by the pope. After Clare's death and*
- *canonization, this "Second Franciscan Order" became*
- *known as the Order of Saint Clare.*
-     *The many women and men who had decided to*
- *adopt lives of penance in response to the preaching of*
- *Francis and his brothers while still living "in the world"*
- *also received greater organization when, in 1221,*
- *Cardinal Ugolino drew up a "memorial of what is pro-*
- *posed for the Brothers and Sisters of Penance living in*
- *their own homes." Among its provisions was a prohibi-*
- *tion against carrying arms and avoiding oaths. Because*
- *the penitents often met at Franciscan churches and*
- *sought out the brothers as spiritual advisors, a more for-*
- *mal association with the Lesser Brothers developed over*
- *the course of the thirteenth century, giving rise to the*
- *name of "Third Order" Franciscans.*

• • •

Plagued with growing ill-health, Francis withdrew more and more from active involvement with the Order's affairs, spending most of his time in the hermitages of central Italy. The experience of the stigmata in September 1224, when the wounds of Jesus' passion burst out on his body, led him to a deep surrender to God's will and a sense of reconciliation. Meanwhile, Brother Elias, working closely with Cardinal Ugolino, continued to work at fostering the involvement of the brothers in the church's ministry. The growing prominence of clerics in the Order was evident in the fact that bishops were beginning to assign small churches to the brothers; in 1224 the Order was allowed to have oratories in all its residences for the celebration of the Eucharist. The following year the pope gave those friars going to Muslim countries extensive sacramental faculties, but in so doing, singled out those roles only an ordained priest could perform. He even dispensed such brothers from key provisions of their rule—such as the ban against using money—in light of the demands of their mission. Accepting a pastoral ministry on behalf of the church was beginning to determine the shape of Franciscan life.

In the summer of 1226, as Francis' health was deteriorating, he composed "an admonition and exhortation" to his brothers which he called his *Testament*. In it, he attempted to recall them to the fundamental inspiration of the movement, reminding the brothers that they were to remain "simple and subject to all." In that spirit, he urged them not to accept any churches or dwellings unless they were truly appropriate for poor men, nor to seek letters of protection from the papal court. He returned to Assisi, dying at the Portiuncula on the evening of October 3, 1226.

Since he had only been appointed to his office by Francis, Elias immediately summoned a general chapter to meet at the Portiuncula the following Pentecost (1227) to choose a new general minister. Although Elias was seemingly the odds-on favorite, the assembly elected instead John Parenti, minister of Spain since 1219, who had been a prominent judge before entering the brotherhood. Meanwhile, earlier that spring, Pope Honorius III had also died; his successor was none other than Cardinal Ugolino, who took the name Gregory IX. Soon after his election, the new pope moved energetically to implement an intense program of reform for both church and society in northern Italy, enlisting local bishops in this effort and promising them the assistance of good men "powerful in action and in preaching."

Gregory saw the Lesser Brothers as an integral part of this campaign to reform Christian society. There is no doubt that he was deeply attached to Francis and his movement, but at the same time he wished to channel it into the service of the church. What better way of recognizing both the legitimacy and potential of the new order than to canonize its founder? Gregory moved quickly to achieve this goal. Even as the process of investigation into Francis' sanctity was still underway, Gregory was making plans to construct a basilica to house his remains. The commune of Assisi donated a hill outside the walls of the city as a site for the church, and in April 1228, the pope sent out a letter to all Christian faithful to drum up donations for the project. Gregory appointed Elias, whom he had come to trust over the years, to oversee the building project. And so, on July 16, 1228, only twenty months after his death, Francis of Assisi was proclaimed a saint. The document announcing this event employed militant imagery from the books of Judges to describe Francis as a new fighter on behalf of the church against its enemies. One of the brothers, Thomas of Celano, a skilled Latinist, was commissioned by the pope to write a *legenda,* or official biography, to introduce the new saint to the wider church.

Work on the new basilica, which was the property of the Holy See, progressed at lightning speed; by the time of the next general chapter in 1230, the lower church was essentially completed, and the body of Saint Francis was joyfully transferred to its final resting place in a crypt beneath the main altar. But this moment of celebration was eclipsed by the deep divisions unmasked by the chapter itself. The brothers found they were in profound disagreement on some fundamental issues. What authority should be given to Francis' last *Testament*? How much freedom did superiors have in interpreting seemingly restrictive provisions of the Rule? Unable to reach consensus themselves, the chapter sent a delegation to Pope Gregory; among them was Anthony, who had served as minister of the friars in the critical region of northern Italy for the previous three years, where he had considerably advanced the pope's reform agenda. Gregory's decisions on the disputed issues, solemnly promulgated in the bull *Quo Elongati* (1230), were those of a principled but flexible jurist. He ruled that the *Testament*, although certainly inspirational, did not have juridical force as it had never been approved by a chapter. With regard to the other disputed issues, the pope treated the Rule as he would any other legal text having an existence independent of the intent of its original author. Most importantly, he interpreted the Rule's strict prohibition of the use of money in a way that allowed laypersons to accept monetary donations on behalf of the

The papal altar in the lower basilica of San Francesco, Assisi, dedicated in 1230. The tomb of Saint Francis lies under this altar.

friars for construction purposes or obtaining necessary items. This provided a certain measure of security so that the brothers might be free to engage in apostolic ministry.

Meanwhile, Anthony returned to full-time preaching, settling outside Padua, a major papal ally, at the small church of the friars there. Anthony was asked by the commune to be its official lenten preacher in 1231; he set up a grueling schedule for himself, preaching daily at various stations throughout the city, hammering home the penitential call for true conversion. In a particular way, he called for achieving a truly Christian society by reconciling feuding political factions and establishing social justice. At his urging, the commune passed a measure that provided relief for people who had fallen into debt. Exhausted, Anthony retired to a small hermitage outside of town, dying suddenly on June 13.

Anthony's ascent to sainthood was even more meteoric than Francis'. The citizens of Padua demanded that "their saint" be canonized, and on May 30, 1232, less than a year after his death, Gregory IX announced that this "Ark of the Covenant" and "Hammer of Heretics"—because of Anthony's profound knowledge of Scripture and defense of orthodox teaching—was now among the saints of the church. In so doing, no doubt the pope intended to reward a staunch ally, but also to send a message to the Lesser Brothers. After all, did their Order really deserve a second saint so soon? Dominic had died in 1221, five years before Francis, and had not yet been canonized—that would not happen until 1234. But Gregory wished to point out to the Lesser Brothers at this critical moment of their history that in addition to their founder, they could aspire to another model of holiness. One could be a devout Lesser Brother and at the same time be a priest serving the pastoral needs of the church. The Franciscans now had two saints, Francis and Anthony, who symbolized two strains that would exist, sometimes in tension, among them from that time forward.

CHAPTER FOUR

Evident Usefulness
to the Church

n 1232, Brother Elias again assumed leadership of the Lesser Brothers, John Parenti having resigned at the Pentecost chapter. The brotherhood was literally exploding with new members and penetrating the most far-flung areas of Christendom. Now, in addition to thirteen provinces in Italy, there were five in what is now France and Belgium, four in the Germanic language territories, three in the Iberian peninsula, two in the Atlantic Isles and one in the Crusader States. If any one individual could be singled out in the story of this remarkable expansion, it would be John of Pian del Carpine (c. 1180–1252), a native of a small town near Perugia who had entered the brotherhood in its early years. A powerful preacher, he accompanied Caesar of Speyer on the expedition to Germany in 1221. John's organizational abilities were soon evident, and in 1227 he was chosen to replace John Parenti as minister of the brothers in Spain, where his successful leadership in implanting the Order led to a division of the territory into three provinces. In 1232, Elias sent him back to Germany as minister of the new province of Saxony. Once again John set to work, organizing the friars' expansion eastward into Bohemia, Hungary and Poland, and northward into

Denmark and Norway. He adopted a strategy of establishing close relationships with the ruling families of these nations, and when he left office in 1239, a number of new provinces had been established there.

In most cases this breathtaking expansion is undocumented, but in the case of both Germany and England, we are fortunate in possessing detailed contemporary chronicles. Thomas of Eccleston wrote his account of the *Coming of the Lesser Brothers to England* in about 1255, which provides a striking illustration of the life and ministry of the friars in that country. It was the general chapter of 1224 that decided an expedition should be launched to England. Most of the nine brothers selected for this mission—four clerics and five lay—were already active in northern Europe. Four were natives of Italy, including their leader, the deacon Agnellus of Pisa, who was part of the second mission sent to France in 1219, where he served as custodian or regional superior of the friars around Paris.

Louis IX of France (1214-1270), from a contemporary depiction. King of France from 1228 to his death, Louis was the paradigm of the devout Christian ruler and a great benefactor of the young Franciscan Order. Although traditionally venerated as a patron of the Brothers and Sisters of Penance (Third Order Franciscans), Louis probably never formally became a member. He was canonized in 1297.

The group arrived at Dover in September, 1224, and headed for Canterbury, where they were received first by the monks at the cathedral and then stayed at a hospice for priests before finding lodging in the basement of a school house. Meanwhile, four of them went on to London, where they stayed with the Dominicans until a house was rented for them by the sheriff. But once again, two of these brothers pushed on to Oxford, where they also found a small house. These movements indicate a deliberate strategy, for within just six weeks of their arrival, the Franciscans had established bases in the ecclesiastical, commercial and intellectual centers of the country. This tactic certainly paid off in terms of recruitment, as the growth of the Order in England was nothing short of phenomenal. Within six years Franciscans were able to settle in a dozen other English towns. By 1235 they had also made their first foundations in Wales (Llanfaes) and Scotland (Roxburgh). Twenty years after that, Thomas would note that "there were 1,242 brothers living in some 49 places"—this in an island of only three million inhabitants.

Friars from England also crossed over to Ireland, apparently settling in Dublin in the late 1220s, but quickly spreading south to Kilkenny and Cork. An independent Irish province was organized at the chapter of 1230, the first minister being Richard of Ingworth, who had been one of the first pioneers in England. When he left office in 1239, there were probably seven Franciscan foundations in Ireland, confined for the most part to the coastal areas controlled directly by England or by Anglo-Norman lords.

But Thomas's treatise does not simply recount an amazing story of expansion; it also illustrates the rapid internal transformation the Franciscans were undergoing, as the trends already evident in the 1220s accelerated in the following decades. In the words of historian Duncan Nimmo, the Order was rapidly becoming "clerical, educated, urban and conventual. Each characteristic spelt modification of the fraternity's primitive pattern."

The figures who dominate Thomas's account of the English province are clearly the clerics: the preachers, confessors and lecturers of theology essential for a fruitful pastoral ministry that was increasingly identified by both the laity and the hierarchy as the

Order's *raison d'être*. Roger of Wendover, a monk of St. Alban's Abbey, in the early 1230s described the Lesser Brothers as an "Order of preachers...dwelling in cities and towns in groups of seven to ten, going forth from their houses during the days, preaching the word of life throughout the villages and in parish churches."

A number of friars were already occupying a prominent place in the church's pastoral ministry. Pope Gregory appointed several as penitentiaries—official confessors of the papal curia. Following in the path blazed by Anthony of Padua, friars like Leo of Perego and Gerard of Modena—who with Anthony had been members of the delegation which approached Gregory in 1230—played a key role preaching in the revival movement known as Great Devotion, which spread like a prairie fire through the cities of northern Italy in 1233. In Parma, thousands swarmed to hear Gerard's fiery sermons. Drafted by the commune to revise its statutes, he prescribed legisla-

The construction of the Upper Basilica of San Francesco in Assisi was completed in 1253. As the "head and mother" church of the Franciscan Order, it became one of the great pilgrimage centers of medieval Christianity.

tion promoting social justice and against heresy. Gregory IX in fact was encouraging friars to assume such leadership roles to bring about a more thorough Christianization of society under papal auspices. The pope had already commissioned a number of friars, such as William of Cordele, to whip up enthusiasm and donations for a new crusade. In 1237, Gregory explicitly identified the Lesser Brothers with the pastoral reform agenda of Lateran IV, stating that the Franciscans were founded to spread the Gospel of Christ, a goal realized specifically through their preaching against heresy and reconciling sinners through confession.

But taking on such important ministries demanded that friars be well-educated. Francis' granting Anthony permission to teach Scripture to the brothers in Bologna was not a unique situation; similar moves were also taking place in northern Europe. During Agnellus's time in Paris, the Lesser Brothers adhered to the pattern of life they followed in Italy, dwelling outside the city in a small house belonging to the Benedictine abbey at St. Denis, from which they journeyed into town to work and preach. Their radical gospel life soon proved attractive to many young intellectuals. Early in 1224 several masters of theology joined them, among whom was an Englishman, Haymo of Faversham (c. 1180–1244). Haymo already enjoyed a considerable reputation as a preacher, so he gained prominence among the Lesser Brothers almost immediately, becoming custodian in Paris, and serving in the delegation that approached Pope Gregory in 1230 for clarifications of the Rule.

Haymo and these other masters began instructing the brothers in theology, but the Order soon realized that in light of its rapidly expanding numbers, it could not rely simply on men who already possessed an education. The Minors would have to develop more systematic means to educate its members. And so, in 1230, through the generosity of King Louis IX, the friars began construction of a large house in the Latin Quarter of the city so they could take advantage of the academic resources of the University of Paris. In 1236, they scored a remarkable coup when a prominent master of the theology faculty, the Englishman Alexander of Hales (c. 1180–1245), entered the brotherhood, transferring his chair to the friars' residence, thus making the Franciscan school an integral part of the university.

England followed a similar pattern. When, in 1229, the friars in Oxford were able to obtain a larger house, Agnellus decided to open a school. He had the great fortune of securing a distinguished theologian, Robert Grosseteste (c. 1175–1253), the first chancellor of the university, to serve as its lecturer. When Grosseteste became bishop of Lincoln in 1235, he was succeeded by several other secular priests until one of his students, Adam Marsh (c. 1200–1259) became the first Franciscan master in 1243. Similar to Paris, the Franciscan school at Oxford, known as Greyfriars, became a constituent part of the university.

Talented friars from the entire Order were soon assigned to Oxford and Paris to obtain the best theological education available at the time. After four years, a brother could be qualified as a bachelor to teach Scripture to the brothers in the larger friaries throughout the Order. A few brothers went on to pursue higher studies in order to gain recognition as masters of theology, enabling the Franciscans to establish their own university-level study centers in other places such as Bologna, Montpellier and Cologne. Within a few years, Franciscan friars were joining their Dominican brethren at the forefront of contemporary theological scholarship.

The pastoral ministries of the friars also meant that they increasingly gravitated to population centers to afford them maximum public availability. It is clear from the early chronicles that the Minors in England and Germany were largely urban from the start. And in Italy, the brothers increasingly abandoned the leper hospices and other shelters on the outskirts, moving within the towns themselves. In 1236, for example, the Archbishop of Ravenna explained that the friars in Bologna had been assigned a church inside the city walls because their former place was too remote, creating serious difficulties for "clerics and scholars who wish to attend classes and sermons, as well as for the citizens at large, who want to go to the brothers to make their confession and to hear the Word of God." In most cases, the natural place for the friars to settle was in the newer, less desirable quarters of expanding towns where land was cheaper. In London, for example, the friars eventually located by Newgate, just outside the city walls on "Stinking Lane," which owed its unsavory name to the proximity of the city's slaughter houses.

As the Minors began to obtain their own churches, the urban setting led them to adopt a simpler version of the typical conventual pattern for a religious house: a quadrangle formed by the church on one side, with a chapter-house (meeting room), refectory (dining room), dormitory and workrooms forming the other sides, arranged around a covered cloister walk. Such an arrangement afforded the friars a certain amount of privacy from the noisy urban surroundings for their life of prayer. But it also meant that they quickly adopted a typical conventual routine, with their daily life organized around the regular celebration of the Liturgy of the Hours and the Eucharist.

• • •

- **FRANCISCAN CONTRIBUTION TO THE CATHOLIC LITURGY**
- *In the Middle Ages, there was no uniform liturgy in*
- *Western Catholicism, but rather many variations from*
- *diocese to diocese. Even in the city of Rome, the great*
- *papal basilicas followed different rituals. As an itinerant*
- *brotherhood spreading throughout Christendom, the*
- *Lesser Brothers needed a uniform liturgy. And so*
- *Francis' Rule of 1223 stipulated that his brothers were to*
- *use the worship books of the clerics who worked in the*
- *papal court. This liturgy intended for busy priests was*

- *further refined under Haymo of Faversham in the 1240s*   •
- *in light of the needs of the Order. The Franciscans'*   •
- *streamlined version of the Roman missal and breviary*   •
- *spread rapidly throughout the Western church and was*   •
- *eventually adopted by the diocese of Rome itself.*   •

•   •   •

The role that the Franciscans were now playing in the larger church is clearly indicated by a story which began to circulate about this time (depicted on this book's back cover) which claimed that some days before Francis' arrival in Rome to seek the approval of Innocent III, the pontiff had a terrifying dream in which the Lateran Basilica began toppling down about him when suddenly a poorly clad little man appeared who began propping it up, averting its collapse. And so, a few days later as the skeptical pope was listening to Francis' request, it dawned on him that this unkempt person standing before him was in fact that man he had seen in his dream. Innocent then realized that Francis' brotherhood would rescue the church from the dangers that threatened it.

Ironically, it was still a lay brother who was presiding over all this development, Brother Elias. He owed his position not simply to his considerable natural abilities, but to his personal friendship with both Saint Francis and Pope Gregory. However, dissatisfaction was brewing against his paternalistic, one-man style of leadership, concentrated in northern Italy and the provinces beyond the Alps, where the new trends were most pronounced. A *coup d'etat* was finally orchestrated by some of the prominent clerics of the Order, led by Haymo of Faversham. They presented a list of allegations to the pope, who reluctantly forced Elias to call a general chapter in 1239. There turned out to be enough substance to these complaints for Gregory to suggest that he resign. When Elias refused to do so, the pope deposed him. The chapter chose as his successor Albert of Pisa, most recently minister of England, the first priest to govern the Order.

However, Albert died within a year, to be succeeded by Haymo himself, the first general minister who was not a member of the early brotherhood in Italy.

The administrations of Albert (1239–1240) and Haymo (1240–1243), although brief, were responsible for what their contemporaries recognized as a thoroughgoing "reformation" of the Lesser Brothers. An ambitious set of constitutions was framed, largely modeled on the Dominicans', which gave the Order a more sophisticated governmental system. The new regulations made sure there would never be another general who enjoyed the power held by Elias. From now on supreme authority was vested in the general chapter held at regular three-year intervals, to which the general minister was held accountable. Furthermore, he could no longer appoint the provincial ministers; from now on they would be chosen by the provincial chapters. But more importantly, these constitutions officially committed the Order to the clericalized version of its mission that was becoming increasingly dominant in practice. Legislation was drawn up severely restricting the type of candidate the Order would accept. Prime consideration was to be given to "useful men" whose previous training equipped them for the pastoral ministries valued by the

Roger Bacon (c. 1214–1292), as depicted in the Oxford University Museum. Roger was already an established master in the arts faculty at the University of Paris when he became a Franciscan in about 1257. Besides fostering research in various scientific fields, his empirical approach led him to advocate a thorough grounding in ancient languages as a basis for biblical study.

church. Candidates fit only for performing domestic work were to be an exception. Furthermore, non-clerics were almost entirely excluded from higher offices in the Order. The original ideal of a brotherhood open to any and all who wished to convert their life according to gospel values was thus substantially modified.

However, it is important to keep in mind that despite all these changes, the Minors still remained strikingly different from both the diocesan clergy and traditional religious orders. While both of these enjoyed substantial incomes from their tithes and endowments, the Lesser Brothers refused to accept such things. Their only livelihood was the practice of the apostles: accepting what people freely offered them in return for their work. Even then, the only donations they accepted were food, clothing and other necessities, not money. When the brothers were given a church, they surrendered any tithes and real estate holdings that came with it. Furthermore, if they did receive a church as a base of operation, it simply served as a gathering place for people drawn to their services, not a canonical parish with its structures of clerical authority over the laity. In all of these ways, the Franciscans continued to preserve a good deal of their role as outsiders to the ecclesiastical system, standing instead with ordinary people who worked for a living.

There was, however, a sizeable party among the friars who believed that in light of the many apostolic tasks the Order had taken on, they had still not modified their way of life enough. Their sentiments found a voice in the new general minister Crescentius of Iesi (1244–1247). He sought a broader interpretation of the Rule from the new pope, Innocent IV (1241–1254), who ruled in the bull *Ordinem Vestrum* (1245) that local guardians might ask the lay agents allowed by Gregory IX to collect money alms not only to meet the immanent necessities of the brothers, but for any purchases they might deem useful. This decree also resolved a legal issue that many critics of the Order had raised: Just who owned the buildings and other belongings the Minors were accumulating, since their Rule specifically forbade them to possess anything? The pope swept such objections aside, decreeing that unless benefactors had reserved ownership for themselves, all the friars' goods were the property of the Holy See. Innocent also intervened in the life of the Order by his decision to appoint a significant number of Franciscans as bishops, a practice begun by Gregory IX in 1241 when, to resolve a disputed election, he allowed the selection of Leo of Perego, then provincial minister of Lombardy, as Archbishop of Milan. Perhaps more ominously, Innocent also began designating Franciscans to act as inquisitors to root out heresy. Both of these offices wielded great power over the lives of other Christians and were thus viewed by many friars as inimical to their vocation to be "simple and subject to all."

The new developments raised voices of protest from the more conservative segment of the Order. When in 1244 Crescentius notified friars who had known Francis personally to contribute more edifying material about the founder, he received a *florilegium* of stories from three of Francis' close companions, Leo, Rufino and Angelo, that effectively offered a critique of current trends in the Order that they saw as compromising its identity as "lesser brothers." These brothers evidently hoped that recalling the example of Francis might provide an authentic witness to the fundamental values of the brotherhood. Thomas of Celano made use of this material in a second memoir on the life of Francis, *The Remembrance of the Desire of a Soul,* submitted to the general chapter in 1247.

That chapter chose a general minister who shared many of these values, John of Parma. Possessing both strong convictions and a charismatic personality, John attempted to steer the Order away from the policies of his predecessor, and was hailed by those friars who wished to preserve the Order's identity as poor, humble brothers. However, John was also fully committed to the pastoral commitments the friars had taken on, and to further them, in 1250 he requested that Innocent grant the Order's churches conventual rights, among which was the permission to bury lay people there, thus enabling the friars to accede to the wishes of its devoted benefactors. That same year, the pope assigned a prominent Roman church, Santa Maria in Aracoeli on the Capitoline Hill, to the Lesser Brothers as a fitting seat of their expanding presence at the center of the church.

These increasing privileges fueled the resentment that many secular clergy held against the new mendicant orders. In the early years, it had been their radically different way of life that had made the Franciscans suspect. Now that they had settled down, adopting more of the familiar patterns of religious life, it was their ever-increasing involvement in ecclesial ministry that was causing tensions. As the friars came to have their own churches, many pastors complained that they were siphoning off a good part of their congregations—with their donations. The University of Paris became a flash point for this discontent in 1252, when the secular masters in the school of theology attempted to curtail the role of the Dominicans and Franciscan masters. The squabble escalated, culminating in the expulsion of the mendicants from the theology faculty in 1253. Although Pope Innocent IV strongly supported the friars, the secular masters preferred to shut down the school in protest rather than readmit the friars to their ranks.

However, a surprise weapon was put into the hands of the seculars when early in 1254 a young Franciscan bachelor at the university, Gerardo of Borgo San Donnino, published a tract based on the writings of an apocalyptic seer, the abbot Joachim of Fiore (c. 1135–1202). In his novel interpretation of the book of Revelation, Joachim had foreseen salvation history moving to a time of fulfillment on earth with an "age of the Spirit," which would be born out of the pangs of a great tribulation in which the Antichrist would be loosed in the world. As in such times of peril in the past, however, Joachim prophesized that God would raise up "spiritual men" to defend the church, this time in the form of two new orders that would lead God's people through these trials to the promised fulfillment. Naturally, there were a number of Franciscans and Dominicans who saw in Joachim's prophecy a messianic reference to themselves. One of the friars caught up in these Joachite speculations was none other than the general minister, John of Parma, who had stated that it was especially the Lesser Brothers' poverty that marked them out as the promised spiritual men. Such ideas took a radical turn with Brother Gerardo's treatise, which claimed that in the impending age of the Spirit, the structures of the institutional clerical church would wither away, to be supplanted by a charismatic gospel community guided by the friars.

Gerardo's work was immediately pounced upon by the secular masters as proof that the friars were indeed an apocalyptic force, but rather as agents of the Antichrist. Their leader, William of St. Amour, argued that the Dominicans and Franciscans were undermining the church's very constitution, by which the pastoral care of the faithful was entrusted to the bishops and their clergy, not to religious, who were supposed to "leave the world" for a life of prayer and contemplation. Innocent IV grew alarmed: On November 21, 1254 he issued a bull *Etsi Animarum*, which severely restricted the friars' privileges. From now on, Innocent ruled, they could no longer admit laity to their services on Sundays, they could not hear the confessions of laypeople without the permission of their parish priest, and any laypersons who wished to be buried in the friars' church still had to pay the customary fees to their own parish. This decree dealt a body blow to the friars' ministry.

However, two weeks later Innocent was dead. The Franciscans were most fortunate in his successor: Cardinal Rainaldo di Jenne, nephew of Gregory IX and protector of the Order for the past quarter-century, who took the name of Alexander IV (1254–1261). He immediately annulled Innocent's restrictions and restored the friars' former privileges. However, the theological storm provoked by the Joachite element in the Order had to be quelled. Alexander appointed a papal commission to examine Gerardo's writings; these were condemned and the rash friar was sentenced to perpetual imprisonment, where he languished until his death in 1276. A more prominent Franciscan was also caught up in the scandal. John of Parma, the general minister, was tarred with the brush of suspect Joachite ideas, and the pope quietly asked him to step aside, which he did at the next general chapter in Rome in 1257. The chapter asked John to suggest a worthy candidate to succeed him; he proposed Bonaventure of Bagnoregio (c. 1221–1274), regent master of the Franciscan school of theology in Paris.

Bonaventure proved more than equal to the task. A native of Italy, he had gone to Paris as a young man to study in the arts faculty of the university. There he was impressed by the Lesser Brothers' growing intellectual prominence, and entered the Order in Paris about 1242, where he had been stationed ever since as both a student and professor. Paris was probably the most international house of the Order, now some thirty thousand members strong. Since all the provinces generally maintained at least two students there, it was a good place to stay in touch with developments throughout the brotherhood, at least from the perspective of its clerical elite. Furthermore, as leader of the friars' debates with the secular masters of the university over the past several years, Bonaventure had articulated a convincing apologia for Franciscan life and ministry.

During his long tenure as general minister (1257–1274), Bonaventure manifested vigorous yet conciliatory leadership. An able defender of the Order, he labored hard to maintain and strengthen the pastoral privileges which earlier pontiffs had conceded to the friars. Convinced that the Lesser Brothers filled a providential role in the history of salvation, he argued that their unique role as evangelical preachers in the church was based on their imitation of Christ and his apostles as poor, gospel men. Indeed, it is fair to say that Bonaventure charted the fundamental direction of the Order for years to come. He systematically codified the general constitutions governing the fractious brotherhood, which were approved at the chapter of Narbonne in 1260. He then was asked to compose a new *Life of St. Francis;* his elegant treatment—which attempted to harmonize contending views of the Order's founder—became the official biography in 1266, thus shaping the image of Francis for future generations of his followers.

Bonaventure managed to be on good terms with all of the popes during his administration, who often sought his advice. Finally, Gregory X (1271–1276) named him a cardinal in 1273 to help organize an ecumenical council he had summoned to reinvigorate crusading efforts and achieve union with the Eastern church. When the Council met at Lyons in 1274, Bonaventure's diplomatic abilities were a factor in accomplishing, at least on paper, a reunion with the church of Constantinople. However, another factor was also at work in the council's agenda: a new theological critique mounted against the mendicant orders of the late 1260s at the University of Paris. A sizeable party among the bishops at the council used these points to again raise objections against the ministerial privileges of the friars. Bonaventure joined Dominican leaders in deflecting their attempts. Although in its last session the council did pass a decree suppressing a number of new mendicant orders that had sprung up in recent decades, it explicitly exempted the Friars Preacher and Friars Minor "because of their evident usefulness to the universal Church." Bonaventure himself did not live to see the triumph of his efforts; he had died suddenly at Lyons several days before. But from now on it was clear that Francis' brothers would remain an important element of the fabric of Catholicism.

CHAPTER FIVE

Crisis of Identity

O n February 22, 1288, Brother Jerome of the Order of Lesser Brothers was enthroned as supreme pontiff, taking the name of Nicholas IV. Jerome was born in 1227, the year after Francis' death; his career is a striking testimony of how quickly the Lesser Brothers had moved from being questionable social outcasts to bulwarks of the institutional church. It also indicates the social mobility that the democratic Lesser Brothers could provide a bright young cleric. In contrast to the typical pope from an old aristocratic family, Jerome had middle-class origins in the rather obscure provincial town of Ascoli Piceno. He had entered the Franciscans as a young man and gained a good education, laboring with great success in the Balkans, eventually becoming minister of the friars in Dalmatia. Due to his linguistic skills, Jerome was tapped for a number of sensitive missions, eventually being selected by Gregory X in 1272 to head an embassy to Constantinople to negotiate union with the Eastern church. When the general chapter met in Lyons just prior to the council, he was the obvious choice to succeed Bonaventure as general minister. But Jerome did not serve long in that capacity, as he too was named a cardinal in 1279.

As pope, Nicholas continued his long interest in the East by send-
ing missionaries to evangelize China. This effort had actually begun
some years previously in response to the tremendous threat posed to
Christendom by the rise of the Mongol Empire. Earlier in the century,
the nomadic Mongol-Turkic tribes of central Asia, united by Genghis
Khan, had launched a wave of conquest, eventually overcoming northern China and advancing against the Muslim and Christian peoples
toward the West. Their fast-moving armies offered peoples in their
path a stark alternative: surrender immediately or be slaughtered. In
1240, they sacked Kiev and ravaged Poland and Hungary. However,
the next year their forces pulled back; Pope Innocent IV, as leader of
Western Christendom, decided in 1245 to approach the Great Khan
with the hopes of warding off future attacks.

The pope named as envoy that intrepid old missionary, John of
Pian del Carpine, who set off with a friar companion early in 1246. In
Kiev they were mounted on swift Mongolian ponies and in 106 days
galloped some three thousand miles across Asia on the great "Silk
Road" to the court of the Great Khan Kuyuk. Although John's

*Niccolo and Maffeo Polo present Kublai Khan's request for missionaries to
Gregory X.*

embassy was unsuccessful, he brought back invaluable information on the peoples of the Far East which he published in his *History of the Mongols*. John especially noted the Mongols' openness to all religions. Indeed, although most were still shamanists, virtually every religion had found converts among them, from Buddhism and Taoism to Islam and Chaldean Christianity (regarded as Nestorian heretics by the Orthodox and Catholic Churches). An intriguing prospect began to emerge: If the Mongols could be converted, then the Muslims of the Middle East would be caught between the pincers of two great Christian forces. In 1253, Louis IX sent another Franciscan, William of Rubruck (c. 1220–1295), who had accompanied him on crusade, to the Mongol court to accomplish this very purpose. Once again, the friars did not achieve their goal but did open up diplomatic and commercial channels.

It was the Mongols who made the next initiative. Kublai Khan (1215–1294) sent requests for missionaries to Gregory X through the merchant Polo brothers and, then, later in the 1270s, sent a Nestorian Christian bishop as ambassador to Rome. In response, Nicholas IV decided to make a concerted effort to evangelize the very heart of the Mongol Empire. He selected John of Montecorvino (1246–1328), a friar who had for some years been active as a missionary in the western part of the Mongol dominions. John set out in 1289, traveling by way of India where he preached for over a year, finally reaching Beijing in 1294. Although Kublai had just died, the new Khan placed no obstacles in his way. By 1305, John was able to convert six thousand to Christianity and build a church opposite the imperial palace. He

John of Montecorvino, first missionary to China.

familiarized himself enough with the native language to translate the New Testament and Psalter into Mongol. Letters describing his success eventually managed to reach Rome; Clement V ordained other friars as bishops and, upon their return to China, consecrated John as Archbishop of Beijing in 1308.

This first Catholic mission in China continued for the next five decades. Fascinating details about the peoples of Asia were transmitted back to Europe by Brother Odoric of Pordenone (1286–1331), who recounted his truly amazing ten-year journey through India, Sri Lanka, Sumatra, Java, Borneo and China (where he spent three years), returning overland via Tibet across central Asia to Europe. However, the Franciscan mission in the East depended on the patronage of the tolerant Mongol overlords. When the native Chinese eventually rose up in revolt in the 1360s, the new Ming dynasty adopted a "closed door" policy toward foreigners. Furthermore, the Turkic tribes of central Asia decided to accept Islam, thus blocking the "Silk Road" to Europeans. These developments thus condemned Christianity in China to extinction.

Nicholas IV also gave definitive legal identity to the vast movement of the Brothers and Sisters of Penance, which had grown up as

Odoric of Pordenone and his companions setting off on their journey to Asia, c. 1316. Two Dominicans who accompanied him as far as India are clearly identifiable by their black preaching capes.

a result of Francis' call for all men and women to convert their lives in light of gospel values. Confraternities of such penitents, who lived in their own homes, engaging in secular occupations, had received a form of life from Cardinal Ugolino in 1221. Over the years, they had developed a spontaneous informal relationship with the Lesser Brothers, turning to them for spiritual guidance. As the friars gained their own churches, it became natural for the penitents to meet there, and in turn, individual penitents often served as the lay "spiritual friends" whom the friars designated to receive monetary alms on their behalf. As part of the institutional church's desire to establish clerical oversight over lay movements, Innocent IV, in 1247, had attempted to submit the Brothers and Sisters of Penance to visitation by the provincial ministers of the Friars Minor. This move was apparently resisted by both the penitents and the friars. Finally, however, in 1289 Pope Nicholas issued his decree *Supra Montem*, which officially instituted "the Order of penance founded by Blessed Francis," urging bishops to name as visitors to such fraternities a priest from among the Minors. This institutionalized the spiritual bonds of the friars with the penitents, leading the latter to be referred to more and more as "The Third Order of Saint Francis."

During his time in the eastern Mediterranean, Pope Nicholas had witnessed the splendor of Byzantine religious art and so determined to enrich Rome in a similar manner. He employed two talented friars, Jacopo Torriti and Jacopo Camerino, to decorate the apses of both the Lateran Basilica and St. Mary Major's with splendid mosaics. Nicholas also turned his attention to beautifying the Basilica of San Francesco in Assisi and conceived a vast fresco program there to glorify both the church and the Franciscan Order. Although today these frescoes by Giotto and other masters are acclaimed as one of the great wonders of medieval art, they were not universally appreciated at the time. In the early 1300s, a friar, Ubertino of Casale, was denouncing them as "scandalous and monstrous vanities." His reaction was symptomatic of deep divisions emerging among the Franciscans.

Although grander in scale, Nicholas' efforts on behalf of the basilica in Assisi were typical of what Friars Minor were doing in much of Western Europe in the late thirteenth century. Full of confidence and enjoying general public support, they were continually expanding their presence in the church. Pope Martin IV in 1281 fostered this by granting the mendicant orders even more extensive privileges, giving them virtual autonomy from local church authorities to pursue their ministry of preaching and hearing confessions—a friar could even claim the right to preach in a church without the pastor's consent! Wishing to accommodate the throngs flocking to their services, Franciscans in larger cities embarked on ambitious building programs.

In Florence, for example, the brothers had been given a small church, Santa Croce, in the mid-1220s, located in a marshy area beyond the town walls. Over the next decades the city had expanded all around it, so in 1294 the friars, with the aid of some of the commune's wealthiest families, began replacing it with a vast new structure. A few years later, in London, the friars likewise began constructing a massive new church at Greyfriars, some three hundred feet in length, with Queen Marguerite, the second wife of Edward I, as a major benefactor. In both cities, the Franciscans' church rivaled the size of the cathedral itself. Of course, the growing number of friars and their manifold activities dictated larger residences as well: In Florence the Franciscan community numbered about 120 brothers by 1300. And in addition to physical expansion, evidence points to a steady and general rise in the Lesser Brothers' standard of living in the period between 1270 and 1320; although they may not have been wealthy, their houses began to show signs of relative comfort. All of this began putting a strain on the Franciscans' traditional financial arrangements and, more importantly, their reputation as poor gospel preachers.

In 1279, Pope Nicholas III, who had been cardinal protector of the Order prior to his election, issued a detailed papal constitution, *Exiit Qui Seminat*, meant to establish definitively the position of the Friars Minor in the church. The pope based himself on an argument developed by Bonaventure, namely, that by renouncing all owner-ship, not only individually but also in common, Franciscans were fol-lowing in a unique way the path of gospel perfection laid out by Christ himself. He reiterated that the Lesser Brothers simply used the things people had donated for their benefit, which were now the property of the Holy See. He did state, however, that the friars' use of such items could not be unlimited, "to the point of any excess, wealth, or abundance," but had to reflect the simple life to which they had committed themselves.

The problem was that as friars continued to expand their activi-ties, they found it difficult to maintain these official standards. Martin IV had aggravated the situation in 1283 by permitting the friars to appoint a layperson as apostolic syndic, who was in effect a business manager nominated by the friars, with full authority to accept dona-tions and to buy and sell things for them in the name of the Holy See. In many places, these syndics began to accept income-producing properties, something forbidden by the stipulations of *Exiit*. Many outside observers, such as the rival Dominicans, as well as some Franciscans themselves, perceived such developments as rendering the Minors' claim to "own nothing" a legal fiction.

For years, a small but persistent faction among the brothers had expressed misgivings about the abandonment of the friars' primitive pattern of life which they believed threatened essential Minorite val-ues. The strong leadership of John of Parma and Bonaventure had managed to mollify their concerns to some extent by steering a con-ciliatory middle path. Now, with the liberalizing element in the Order seemingly in full control, the rumblings of discontent became more strident. A loose coalition who came to be known as "Spirituals" began to mount a challenge to the direction the Order was taking. Their name probably arose from a key provision in the Rule of 1223 which stated that brothers should always enjoy the freedom to observe the Rule spiritually, even to the point of resisting the commands of superiors that went against it. The zealots considered the *Testament* of Francis a sure guide to this spiritual observance of his gospel life.

The resistance to the liberal trends was most marked in the mountainous areas of central Italy; there, friars continued to dwell in small hermitages, retelling stories about Francis passed on by his early companions. In the province of the Marches, rumors began spreading in the early 1270s that the upcoming Council of Lyons was going to make the Lesser Brothers conform to the practice of other religious orders and own property. A number of friars stated that should it do so, they would refuse to obey; even the pope himself could not dispense them from following the Rule of Francis, as it was a pure expression of the gospel of Christ. These friars were viewed as disruptive by their provincial minister; three who remained particularly intransigent, among them Peter of Fossombrone, later known as Angelo Clareno (c. 1255–1337), were imprisoned as heretics. It was only when a new general minister, Raymond Geoffroi, was elected in 1289, that they were released.

Raymond, a native of Provence, sympathized with the views of a brilliant theologian in his own province, Peter John Olivi (1248–1298), whose outspoken originality on a number of issues had earned him enemies within the Order. Olivi was particularly controversial for his treatment of the distinctive "life according to the Gospel" a Friar Minor pledged to observe. He asserted that this commitment demanded not only the simple renunciation of ownership, but also a "poor use" of things. Thus, Olivi considered a habitually affluent way of life or the construction of grandiose buildings to be a violation of the Franciscan vow of poverty. Olivi had been exiled from his own province as a troublemaker as a result, being assigned to teach in Florence from 1287–1289, but this move permitted his ideas to spread to Italy, thus providing the Italian Spirituals with a theological base for their objections.

During the 1290s the Spirituals became increasingly vociferous, wearing a short, shabby habit as a mark of their primitive observance, insisting on the "poor use" of goods and demanding the right to observe the Rule "to the letter," without any papal interpretations. Because the Spirituals felt that involvement in urban pastoral ministry and academic studies had led to the abuses plaguing the Order, they advocated a withdrawn life in small hermitages conducive to maintaining simplicity and poverty. As one of their spokesmen, the poet Jacopone of Todi (1228–1306), proclaimed: "Paris has demolished Assisi: With all their learning, they've led us down a crooked path."

The Spirituals suddenly found the opportunity to follow their vision with the surprise election as pope in 1294 of an elderly Italian hermit, Peter Murrone, who took the name Celestine V. He allowed a group of Spirituals including Angelo Clareno, to separate from their superiors so they might practice the literal observance of the Franciscan Rule, living in their own hermitages under the canonical umbrella of his own congregation of "Poor Hermits." However, Celestine abruptly abdicated the papal office later the same year. His successor, the ambitious clerical careerist Boniface VIII (1294–1303), viewed the "Poor Hermits" as a disruptive element and withdrew their authorization. Furthermore, he forced the resignation of Raymond Geoffroi, whom he felt was too sympathetic to the Spiritual cause. The new general minister, John of Murrovale, fully agreed with Boniface's position and cracked down on the Spirituals. John also began an investigation into the writings of Olivi; although the Provencal friar died in 1298, his writings were condemned by the general chapter the following year.

However, the Spirituals continued to press their position, gaining a number of prominent sympathizers. Pope Clement V (1305–1314), who had relocated the papal court to Avignon, decided to impose a truce on the contending parties until he could adjudicate the matter. It was at this time that one of the Spiritual leaders, Ubertino of Casale, composed a powerful but inflammatory devotional treatise, *The Tree of the Crucified Life of Jesus*, which in apocalyptic Joachite language portrayed Francis as a prophetic figure, rejected by his own disciples. It was therefore becoming incumbent for his true "spiritual" followers to separate from the "carnal community" of the Order so as not to be complicit in its sins.

A full papal investigation into the Order's internal affairs was carried out between 1309 and 1312. Each side mustered documents and evidence to support its case. The leadership of the Order pled for unity and observance of the official standards; the Spirituals, represented by Ubertino, argued that the Order was in fact not living up to those standards and that therefore a stricter observance should be allowed. Clement's verdict, announced in the bull *Exivi de Paradiso* (1312) offered an eminently reasonable compromise. On the one hand, it represented a victory for the Spirituals, as it acknowledged that many of Ubertino's criticisms were in fact valid. The bull went on to specify areas in which the Order had to tidy up its life. On the other, it urged the Spirituals to submit to their superiors and to obey their day-to-day decisions on practical matters such as clothing, food and buildings. Clement also secured the election of a new general who would be more sympathetic to the Spirituals. A solution seemed to have been reached.

However, in 1314, both the pope and the general minister died. Successors were not chosen for another two years, and during the long vacancy, Clement's compromise unraveled in the face of extremists on both sides. In some provinces, superiors began again to harass the Spirituals. In Tuscany, dissident Spirituals left their friaries to become itinerant preachers; in Provence they seized control of several houses by force.

In 1316, a new pope and general minister were finally elected. The general, Michael of Cesena, faced with virtual anarchy in his ranks, turned to Pope John XXII (1316–1334) for assistance. John, an elderly but determined canon lawyer, moved quickly to bring the Spirituals to heel. In 1317, in the bull *Quorundam Exigit*, he warned the dissidents to submit to their superiors: "Poverty is good, but charity is greater, and obedience is greatest of all." He followed up later in the year by excommunicating all friars—often called *fraticelli* ("little brothers") in Italy—who refused to heed his decree. The Spiritual leaders in Provence were arrested and forced to recant. Four holdouts, judged heretics by the Inquisition for refusing to assent to the pope's commands, were burnt at the stake in Marseilles in 1318. These actions proved to be the death-knell for the Spiritual movement. Their leaders, Angelo Clareno and Ubertino of Casale, fled for sanctuary to Benedictine abbeys; however, they both were eventually forced through fear of the Inquisition to leave, dying as virtual outlaws on the fringes of the institutional church.

But John was not yet finished with the Franciscans. He began to examine more closely the argument underlying the Spirituals' case, namely that they alone were living up to the absolute poverty followed by Christ and Francis, in contrast to the mainstream of the Order—and by implication, the rest of the church—which had abandoned it. The pope determined to challenge this entire theory and so in March, 1322 declared that the issues decided in Pope Nicholas III's decree of 1279, *Exiit Qui Seminat*, would be reconsidered. The Franciscans, gathered at their general chapter in Perugia, were alarmed and spiritedly defended their position, inferring that the pope did not have the power to overturn a binding decree of his predecessor. This show of resistance served only to infuriate Pope John, who in December, 1322, in the apostolic constitution, *Ad Conditorem*, dramatically reversed the entire papal policy of the past century by renouncing dominion over the Order's goods. This effectively cut the ground out from under the Franciscans' claim of being unique among religious orders by owning nothing. Finally, in December, 1323, John capped his revisionist program by flatly denying the doctrine of the absolute poverty of Christ, stating that it was in fact heretical to state that Jesus and the apostles did not own property.

The Franciscan Order—and much of Christendom—were stunned by John's actions; the Emperor Louis IV, who was locked in political conflict with the pope, accused him of heresy. The situation escalated when the emperor invaded Italy in 1327. In this highly charged situation, Michael of Cesena's resolute defense of the Franciscan position caused the pope to confine him to Avignon, refusing to let him attend the upcoming general chapter in Bologna. Fearing imprisonment or worse, Michael, with several other friars, among them the English theologian William of Ockham (c. 1288–1348), fled Avignon in May, 1328, taking refuge with the emperor. They discovered that the chapter had defied Pope John by reelecting Michael; furthermore, Louis had installed a Franciscan, Pietro of Corvaro, as the "true" pope, who took the name Nicholas V. The Friars Minor, who prided themselves on their close relationship with the papacy, seemed headed for open rebellion.

But the tide was flowing against the Franciscan resistance. Support of Louis's invasion of Italy withered away and he retreated to Germany. John, safely ensconced in Avignon, deposed Michael and summoned the provincial ministers loyal to him to meet in chapter in Paris in 1329. They elected a new general minister, Guiral Ot (Gerardus Odonis), like the pope a native of Aquitaine. Eventually, "Nicholas V" submitted to Pope John. Michael of Cesena and William of Ockham, however, persisted in their defiance at the imperial court in Munich until their deaths in the 1340s.

During these tumultuous years most Franciscans, whatever

their own sympathies in the struggles wracking the Order might be, went about their life and ministry. In the British Isles, for example, the bitter Spiritual controversies were not that evident. The English province had from its origins been noted for combining rigorous observance of the Rule with devotion to study; a similar situation existed in Ireland. And so, there were few friars at the extreme ends of the Franciscan spectrum which had given rise to the tensions in Italy and southern France. Indeed, the Franciscans were at the height of their prestige and influence in the British Isles in the later years of the thirteenth century, noted both for their leadership in theological studies and their dedication to popular preaching. Mirroring the growing prominence of the Franciscans in other countries, John Pecham (c. 1230–1292), a professor at the University of Oxford and then minister of England, was named Archbishop of Canterbury in 1279.

It was during these years that the Friars Minor in Ireland expanded significantly into the Gaelic-speaking areas of Ulster and Connacht, outside the pale of English control. Indeed, some Anglo-Irish friars complained about some of their confreres who "in the Irish language spread seeds of rebellion" among the people. These ethnic differences in the province erupted in violence at a chapter in Cork in 1291, when a number of friars were allegedly slain.

It was also in the midst of the Spiritual conflict that the Franciscans gained their third canonized saint. Louis of Anjou (1274–1297) was a son of Charles II, King of Naples, who belonged to a junior branch of the French royal house. Charles had been captured in a battle with Aragon over the control of Sicily; to gain his freedom, he arranged for three of his sons, including Louis, to take his place as hostages. The youths spent seven years in Aragon (1288–1295), where their education was entrusted to several Friars Minor, who put them in contact with Peter John Olivi. Inspired by their ideals, Louis determined to join the Franciscans. Upon his release, he dramatically renounced his rights of inheritance in favor of his brother Robert, entering the Order in 1296. Boniface VIII had already named him bishop of Toulouse. Louis immediately committed half of his revenues to the poor, but died suddenly after only a few months in office. Pope Clement V promoted Louis's cause for sainthood, which was completed in 1317, strikingly demonstrating the strong connection between the papacy, the French monarchy and the Franciscan Order.

Louis's brother Robert, who became King of Naples in 1309, proved to be a great benefactor to the Friars Minor. Their last base in the Holy Land had been lost in 1291 when the city of Acre fell to the Muslims. However, a few brothers managed to lead a tenuous existence within Muslim territory ever since a truce in 1229, living peaceably and placing themselves at the service of Western pilgrims. Finally, King Robert concluded a treaty with the Sultan of Egypt in 1333, through which the property of the Cenacle in Jerusalem was secured for the use of the Lesser Brothers, who were allowed to minister at the Church of the Holy Sepulchre and a number of other holy places. In 1342, Pope Clement VI ratified their role by erecting the Custody of the Holy Land for the friars who served there. Franciscans have remained as the Catholic guardians of these holy places to our own day.

Reform and Division

y 1330, many Franciscans were left both dazed and disillusioned in the wake of the tremendous crisis their Order had just been through. Although they continued to be effective ministers in the church, some wondered what remained of their fundamental ideals. This situation became even more confused when Pope Benedict XII, a Cistercian monk, sensing the lack of standards among the friars, decided in 1336 to force the general chapter to adopt a new set of constitutions. These were a clear break from the Order's tradition. They made little mention of the characteristic Franciscan values of poverty or mission. Instead, the emphasis was on the friars' leading a virtually monastic life, with detailed prescriptions on the observance of silence, the prohibition of meat and the choral recitation of the Divine Office. Although these regulations were modified somewhat by a new set of constitutions in 1354, these still envisioned that the friars would spend most of their lives within the walls of their cloister, exercising their ministry largely within their own church. Strict penalties were enacted against "vagrancy": No friar was to go out into town more than once a week, young ones no more than once a month.

The friars were also creating their own version of Benedictine stability. Rather than being transferred from place to place as had been the previous practice, a Franciscan now generally entered the friary in his home town and remained there—or at least in the surrounding custody—for the rest of his life. This contributed to the Order's becoming deeply entrenched as a constituent unit of local society. In Italy, there was even a neighborhood identification, as the churches of the major mendicant orders became unofficial gathering places for the various quarters of the city. The friars' churches became the preferred burial place for the social elite and, more importantly, the communities themselves were filled with members of the prominent families of the city.

The Order was also taking on attributes of social hierarchy. The local superiors or guardians were assuming prerogatives of abbots, often with their own separate living quarters. Masters of theology also rated their own private rooms and dispensed from attendance at choir, often with a lay brother assigned to them as a personal valet. In this context, it is not surprising that friars competed with each other to get a higher education, as this was seen as the gateway to advancement. Others strove to obtain outside appointments, such as a chaplaincy to an aristocratic family, which would guarantee them a private income. Legislation even had to be enacted to provide for "needy friars" who did not have access to such funds or gifts from their families.

In addition, the great bubonic plague, or "Black Death," that ravaged Europe from 1347–1351 had a devastating effect on the Order. Perhaps 30 to 40 percent of the general population succumbed, but since the Franciscans were concentrated in cities, where sanitation was poor, the effect on them was even more dramatic. Many friars died ministering to the victims of the plague. A Franciscan chronicle states that "scarcely one-third of the brothers of the Order survived." Furthermore, the friars' desire to replenish their ranks in the wake of the plague led them to lower their standards, recruiting immature and unfit candidates who could not live up to the demands of Franciscan life.

It was such factors that gave rise to the stock figure of the friar in late medieval literature, such as in Chaucer's *Canterbury Tales* and Boccaccio's *Decameron*: an affable but unscrupulous fellow, with a taste for good food and wine, intent on milking unsuspecting people for donations, and whose preaching was filled with jokes rather than the gospel. Still, the Order remained popular among a large proportion of the laity. Despite the stereotypes that arose from the bad behavior of some, many friars were still living simply and doing good work. In England for example, an analysis of wills in the late fourteenth century shows that a large proportion of people left bequests to the Franciscans.

Nevertheless, devotion to the ideals of the primitive Franciscan movement remained alive, especially within central Italy. Around the year 1330, many colorful anecdotes about Francis and the early brothers, some of them apocryphal, were collected by a friar in the Marches in a treatise called *The Deeds of Blessed Francis and His Companions*. A vernacular Italian translation, the *Fioretti* (*The Little Flowers of St. Francis*) became immensely popular over the course of the century, shaping the popular image of Francis for generations. Above all, the *Fioretti* stressed that "the glorious Saint Francis was conformed to the blessed Christ in all the acts of his life." This motif was carried to its ultimate expression by Bartholomew of Pisa (d. 1401), who compiled his massive *Book of Conformities of the Life of Blessed Francis with the Life of the Lord Jesus* between 1385 and 1395. This work, which scholar John Fleming aptly labeled "encyclopedic in its ambitions and audacious in its design," attempted to demonstrate the parallels between Francis and Christ to the slightest detail. It received the stamp of approval of the general chapter of 1399 and spread rapidly throughout the Order. Bartholomew's

compilation shaped subsequent Franciscan history because it dissem-
inated many texts, both unofficial biographies and the writings of
Francis himself, which otherwise would have remained unknown.

It was within this context of a literary retrieval of Francis' life that
currents of reform began to circulate in the Franciscan heartland of
central Italy. The center of this movement was the friary in Foligno,
only a few miles from Assisi. This was the home of Angela (d. 1309),
a lay Franciscan penitent and mystic who attracted a group of zealous
friars as disciples; the surrounding hills also offered sanctuary for
bands of *fraticelli*, the followers of Angelo Clareno. Some friars in the
Foligno community began expressing the desire for a reformed
Franciscan life. In 1334, one of them, a priest named John of Valle,
received permission from the general minister, Guiral Ot, to retire
with a few companions to the remote hermitage of Brugliano in the
rugged hill country, so that they might follow "a literal observance of

*The coat of arms of the Franciscan Order—showing the bare arm of Christ
raised over the robed arm of Francis, both with the stigmata, with a cross in
the middle—depicting the total conformity of Francis to Christ.*

the Rule, purely and simply." It is ironic that Guiral would grant such permission in light of the wrenching conflicts the Order had just experienced, as John's agenda simply recreated that of the Spirituals. Historians have suggested that this was Guiral's attempt to mount a flanking movement against the *fraticelli* in a region where they enjoyed a good deal of popular support by creating the opportunity to lead the primitive Franciscan vision within the structures of the Order. In any event, the new reform took root and spread to several other hermitages in the region.

However, its success was short-lived. Unfortunately, some of the reformers began to take an adversarial stance toward the other brothers, adopting the distinctive short habit associated with the Spirituals and strengthening ties with renegade *fraticelli*. In 1351, John's successor, Gentile of Spoleto, appealed to Pope Clement VI for a perpetual guarantee to observe their vision of Franciscan life without any interference from their superiors. This move proved their undoing. In response, the general chapter of 1354 mounted an investigation that indicated heterodox tendencies in the movement, thus securing a decision by Clement's successor to disband the embryonic group.

The dream of a reformed Franciscan life refused to die, however. The man who resurrected it was a humble friar, Paolo Vagnozzi, generally known by his nickname, Paoluccio, or "little Paul." Born in Foligno in 1309, he was related to the aristocratic family of the Trinci who were lords of the city. He entered the Franciscans at the age of fourteen, but took the highly unusual step of choosing the life of a lay brother, devoting himself to domestic chores in the friary and begging for alms. At some point he had joined one of the reformed hermitages, but when they were disbanded in 1354, he had to return to the friary in Foligno, where he endured ridicule. Finally, in 1368, his family connections paid off: his cousin, the lord of Foligno, obtained permission from the general minister for Paoluccio to retire to Brugliano to lead a simple, austere life. Brugliano was in a rugged location, characterized by both rocks and swamps; as a result, the friars adopted small wooden clogs or *zoccoli* as footwear, which would later give rise to the nickname of *zoccolanti* for the Italian Observants. Their way of life revived many of the aspects of the early brotherhood that had been sacrificed in the name of ministerial effectiveness: a focus on contemplative prayer, equality among lay and ordained friars and a genuinely poor life.

This time, the reform movement succeeded largely due to Paoluccio's humble but determined leadership and his strong orthodoxy in confronting the *fraticelli*. In the 1370s, the movement grew rapidly. Pope Gregory XI gave permission for a number of other hermitages to be reserved for the reformers, including the Carceri above Assisi and Greccio, near Rieti. In the 1380s, the movement received a certain measure of autonomy when the general minister made Paoluccio commissary over twelve reformed houses in the two provinces of Umbria and the Marches with permission to receive novices. By the time he died in 1391, there were over twenty friaries in central Italy of what was being called the Observant Reform.

In Spain and France there were similar attempts to return to a lost "golden age" of Franciscan life. In contrast to central Italy, where there was an unbroken tradition of eremitical life, these were literally a "new creation" inspired by friars reading unofficial historical sources such as the *Fioretti*. In Galicia, beginning in 1392, some friars received permission to retreat to rural locations in order to devote themselves more fully to prayer. In the province of Castile, Pedro de Villacreces, a graduate of the University of Salamanca, introduced a form of Franciscan life almost Cistercian in severity. Within their small friaries located in remote areas, Pedro's followers devoted about twelve hours a day to liturgical prayer (Mass and the Divine Office) and private meditation, focused on Scripture and devotional works. As he told them, "I received my master's degree, which I did not deserve, for I have learned more weeping in the darkness of my cell than studying by candle in Salamanca." One of his disciples, Pedro Regalado (1390–1456) became noted for his withdrawn and ascetic life—he fasted on bread and water for most of the year.

Reform currents in France also date from the 1390s, first evident in the friary of Mirabeau in Touraine, which spread over the next two decades to about a dozen other locations. In contrast to the Italian and Spanish Observants, however, the French reformers did not have an eremitical emphasis; rather, their goal was to establish reformed urban communities that followed the Rule of Saint Francis according to the official papal declarations. Since these friars of the "regular observance" were explicitly reacting against the "nonobservant" conditions they saw in the Order, they wanted to obtain a degree of independence from their superiors to enable them to attain their goals.

Perhaps one reason so many independent reform movements were cropping up at this time was due to the fact that there was no realistic hope for reform at the higher levels of the Order due to the Great Western Schism. This disastrous episode in the life of the church originated in a disputed papal election in 1378. Two men—one with his court in Rome, the other in Avignon—each claimed to be the valid pope, thus dividing Western Christendom into rival blocks, largely split on political lines. The situation was reflected within the Franciscan Order, with provinces loyal to each of the papal contenders electing rival general ministers. The Schism continued for three decades, destroying any effective central authority in the Order. In addition, each of the general ministers found their position undermined by the rival popes, as both of them, in an attempt to curry support, were lavishly bestowing dispensations on suppliants.

Although such divided authority naturally tended to promote lax behavior, it could at times favor the cause of reform. Thus, when the French Observants approached the Avignon pope, Benedict XIII in 1407, he granted them exemption from the control of their provincial ministers. However, their situation soon changed. Disgusted with the failure of both the Roman and Avignon popes to heal the Schism, most of the cardinals of both obediences deserted them, and with the support of the principal rulers in Europe, called a council which met in Pisa in 1409. This gathering proceeded to elect a third pope (!)— the Franciscan Peter of Candia, who took the name Alexander V. Alexander, who was backed by the French king, naturally supported the authorities of the Order and so revoked the privileges of the French Observants. However, Alexander died within a year. His successor, John XXIII, although commanding the loyalty of most of Western Christendom, was unable to secure the removal of the other two papal claimants. This led the rulers of Europe to insist that John summon a new Council at Constance in 1414 to put an end to the schism once and for all.

Thus it was that the French Observants took their case to the council, which granted their request, establishing within three French provinces a separate custody for the reformed houses, each governed by a vicar who would be only nominally subject to the provincial minister. However, another, distinct reform movement was also springing up among the French Franciscans. This was initiated by Colette of Corbie (1381–1447), who had likewise secured permission from Benedict XIII to begin a reform of the Franciscan Order. As Colette began to found new monasteries of Poor Clares with the assistance of her confessor, Henry of Baume, she wanted to insure that there would be a community of reformed friars attached to each house to minister to the sisters. Although her goals were similar to those of the French Observants, she refused to have her friars join them since she considered them disobedient due to their separatist attitude. Instead a separate reform congregation grew up in France, subject to the provincial ministers, popularly referred to as "Colettans."

By the 1420s, the various groups calling for "observance" of the Rule were becoming increasingly prominent and could count upon enthusiastic support from the laity. Part of the reason for this was that both the Italian and Spanish reformers at times went out from their hermitages to engage in the popular itinerant preaching that characterized the early years of the Franciscan movement. The best example of this is the career of Bernardine of Siena, the most celebrated preacher of the fifteenth century. Born in the town of Massa Marittima in 1380, Bernardine ("little Bernard") was the only child of aristocratic parents. Orphaned by the age of six, he was raised by relatives in Siena, who provided the bright lad with an excellent education. He had begun to study law when, in 1400, a severe plague broke out in the city; Bernardine and some friends ended up taking charge of the local hospital. Soon after, he determined to offer his life to God, entering the Friars Minor in Siena in 1402. However, he was disappointed by the easygoing life of the community and so received permission to transfer to the Observant hermitage of Il Colombaio.

There Bernardine immersed himself in the Spiritual tradition, including the writings of Peter John Olivi and Ubertino of Casale, in addition to academic theology. Ordained in 1404, he spent the next dozen years based at a small hermitage outside Siena, where he devoted himself to prayer and itinerant preaching.

However, Bernardine felt called to travel further north to preach, where he gained great notoriety after a spectacular series of lenten sermons in Milan in 1418.

Bernardine of Siena carrying the image of the Holy Name of Jesus in a painting by El Greco.

For the next twenty-six years, he was constantly on the move, walking from place to place with sometimes as many as a dozen companions, who assisted him with practical arrangements and hearing confessions. Bernardine's preaching campaigns had a strong puritanical streak, inveighing against the evils of society. One of their features was the "bonfire of the vanities" at which people cast their frivolous luxuries and amusements into the flames. Bernardine also promoted devotion to the Holy Name of Jesus, often carrying with him a banner with its monogram as a symbolic rallying point for people who wished to convert their lives.

In the course of his preaching missions, Bernardine also made efforts to advance his vision of Franciscan reform. During his lifetime, he founded or renewed over three hundred friaries in Italy. Bernardine had an able lieutenant in John of Capistrano (1385–1456). The son of a high-ranking officer in the service of the King of Naples, John received a legal education at the University of Perugia. However, he abandoned his career to enter the Observants in 1415 and soon became an itinerant preacher. John was a driven man with great practical organizational skills; allowing himself only three or four hours of sleep a night, he tirelessly advanced the cause of the reformation of Christian society and of the Franciscan Order.

The growth of the Observants attracted the attention of Pope Martin V (1417–1431). A reformer elected at the Council of Constance, Martin pushed the cause of reform among the Franciscans by extending the privilege enjoyed by the French Observants to those in other countries. Furthermore, in 1428 he annulled John XXII's decree *Ad Conditorem* of 1322, thus allowing any friary which wished to do so to return to the practices spelled out in the earlier papal declarations: namely, to divest itself of its property, turning it over to the Holy See, and putting the management of its financial affairs in the hands of a lay apostolic syndic. In light of this, he asked the Order to embark on a comprehensive reform program at the general chapter of 1430. There the Observants agreed to give up their autonomy under their own vicars in return for the entire Order adopting a set of reform constitutions. Largely composed by John of Capistrano, these called for all friars to observe a minimum standard of poverty by divesting themselves of income-producing property and prohibiting the use of money.

Although the chapter approved the new constitutions, the newly launched reform effort struck the shoals of reality when the provincial ministers returned home to meet strong resistance against them. The general minister therefore approached the pope, who in August 1430 issued the decree *Ad Statum*, which legitimized the rights of local houses to own property and enjoy regular incomes. This decree for the first time officially marked off a "Conventual" party from those friars who wished to be "Observant," dooming the hope for uniform Franciscan standards. In response, the disgruntled Observants demanded that the pope restore their provincial vicars, thus establishing two parallel authority structures throughout the Order. This arrangement was formalized by Pope Eugene IV in 1446; in effect he made the Observants a congregation within the larger Order by granting them their own vicars general—one for the "Ultramontane" provinces north of the Alps, the other for the "Cismontane" provinces in Italy and in Eastern Europe—under their own constitutions. This arrangement would perdure for more than half a century and became even more complex as still other smaller reforms sprang up and obtained their own autonomy. Meanwhile, the Observants gained some important symbolic victories: In 1445, the pope entrusted to them the church of Aracoeli in Rome, the traditional home of the Order's general curia. And in 1450 Bernardine of Siena was proclaimed a saint, the fourth Friar Minor to be canonized, and the first since Louis of Toulouse 130 years previously.

Meanwhile, the Observants were spreading to other countries: to Germany in the 1420s and to eastern Europe in the 1430s. At the same time, the desire to lead a stricter life reached Ireland. Several new friaries were founded, mainly in Irish-speaking areas, and they received their own vicar provincial in 1460. Within a few years, a number of older houses, such as Youghal and Multyfarnam, also joined the Observant reform. The Observants were also introduced into Scotland in the 1460s.

The latter half of the century witnessed a constant rivalry between the two parties in the Order as they competed, often acrimoniously, for vocations and public support. When the theologian Francesco Della Rovere, general minister from 1464–1469, was elected pope as Sixtus IV (1471–1484), he used his position to consolidate the privileges enjoyed by the Order and tried to curtail the Observants; he also proclaimed Bonaventure a saint in 1482. On the other hand, in Spain, the Observants gained the upper hand under the austere Francisco Ximénes de Cisneros (1436–1517). He was a secular priest on a rising career path when in his late forties he renounced his worldly life and joined the Observant friars in Toledo. Despite his desire for a contemplative life, in 1492 Queen Isabella of Castile selected Cisneros as her confessor, which gave him immense influence at court; in 1495 Isabella nominated him archbishop of Toledo and inspector of all religious orders. In that position he applied great political pressure on the Conventual houses in Spain to accept reform, even over papal objections.

Sixtus IV, pope from 1471–1484, was noted both for his great patronage of the arts and his flagrant nepotism (this image of the pope in his court includes several of his nephews). He directed the construction of the Sistine Chapel.

These intramural Franciscan tensions should not cause us to lose sight of one of the major cultural developments of the period, that is, the humanist movement of the Renaissance, which emphasized a return to the sources of Christian faith. Although the majority of the Order's theologians were not particularly original, continuing to work within the Scholastic synthesis of John Duns Scotus, others took a great interest in the new intellectual currents. One of these was Cardinal Cisneros himself, who founded the University of Alcalá de Henares in 1499. There he assembled a team of scholars who compiled the multivolume *Complutensian Polyglot*, in which the biblical text was published in parallel columns in Hebrew, Greek and Latin, with extensive notes. In Italy, the Conventual Luca Pacioli (c. 1445–1517), a mathematician, became a close collaborator of Leonardo da Vinci. His *Summa de Arithmetica* (1494) first described the method known as the double-entry system of accounting.

As the new century dawned, the papacy realized that some final resolution of the nagging Franciscan question was necessary. After several futile attempts to arrive at a legislative solution to the problem, Pope Leo X finally convoked a "most general" chapter, gathering together not only the provincial ministers, but all the Observant vicars and the heads of the other smaller reform branches as well. When the assembly convoked at the church of the Aracoeli in Rome in May 1517, it quickly became mired in fruitless bickering. This led the pope to impose his own solution, announced in the decree *Ite Vos in Vineam* (May 29, 1517). He declared that the representatives of the various reform groups—who now were the majority of the Order—would constitute the legitimate general chapter, and that they alone would have the authority to elect a new general minister. However, they were to give up their separate names and authority arrangements, uniting under a common leadership as "the Friars Minor of Saint Francis of the Regular Observance." The leaders of the reformed friars accordingly elected Christopher of Forli, vicar of the Italian Observants, as general minister. The Conventual minis-ters, shut out of the election, gathered on their own and elected their own general, Anthony Marcello. The pope, hoping they would come around and accept the reform, did not ratify their election until June 12. Then, in the decree *Omnipotens Deus*, he declared that they would constitute a separate congregation, the "Order of Friars Minor Conventual," having their own superiors and free to enjoy their legal privileges and property rights. With this divorce, Francis' brother-hood was no longer one. It has remained divided ever since.

CHAPTER SEVEN

Forging Spiritual Weapons

It would appear that the friars of the Observance emerged triumphant from the events of 1517, in that their "unreformed" brothers who did not choose to live according to the earlier papal standards had been segregated into their own Order. However, the division did not produce the chief goal that Pope Leo had intended, namely, the rallying of all reformed Franciscans around a common ideal. The reason for this was simple: As the Observants had flourished, fully entering the mainstream ministry of the church, their standard of a "regular observance" under the early papal interpretations of the Rule could not satisfy those friars who felt drawn to an eremitical life or a more austere expression of poverty. The "call of the wild" continued to lure Franciscans away from domesticated forms of the gospel life to return to primitive values.

The very year that Leo X decreed the Union, a Spanish friar, Juan Pascual, managed to evade the pope's edict by obtaining permission from the Conventual general minister to maintain a small autonomous group of "Discalced" ("barefoot") Franciscans under his aegis. This, the most austere of reforms within the Franciscan tradition, traced its origins to 1496 when a friar, Juan de Guadalupe

(d. 1506), received permission to follow the Rule according to a "most strict observance." His friars lived a very poor life, wore a distinctive patched habit, refusing even the use of sandals, and exercised a ministry as itinerant preachers. With the union of 1517, they were ordered to join the Observants, which most of them did, forming the province of San Gabriel, but Juan Pascual and his few followers succeeded in remaining separate to assure their distinctive practices. In Italy also, more zealous friars, much in the same spirit as the first Italian Observants, obtained permission to establish so-called houses of recollection or *retiros* where a stricter form of life could be led, although they remained under the jurisdiction of the Observant provincial ministers. When Francisco de los Angeles Quiñones, a disciple of Cardinal Cisneros, was elected general minister in 1523, he encouraged this development in Italy.

The most important of these new reform movements were the Capuchins, who experienced a truly phenomenal growth despite inauspicious origins. Their roots trace back to an Observant friar, Matteo of Bascio, who, at a time of great poverty in the Marches of Italy, began experiencing pangs of dissatisfaction with the comfortable life in his friary at Montefalcone. He secretly left the friary, adopting what he believed was the primitive habit of the Franciscans, with a long pointed hood attached directly to the tunic, and traveled to Rome during the jubilee celebration of 1525. Settling there at a hospital for the incurable sick, he approached Pope Clement VII who gave him oral permission to wear this habit and to engage in itinerant preaching. Two other friars, the blood brothers Ludovico and Raffaele of Fossombrone, also desiring a more primitive form of life, asked their provincial minister, Giovanni of Fano, for permission to join Matteo in a hermitage. When he refused, the three became impatient and left their friary, taking refuge at a Conventual house in Cingoli. Angered, Giovanni approached the Vatican and obtained authority to imprison them as renegades from the Order.

However, the little group was saved due to a powerful protector, Caterina Cybò, Duchess of Camerino, a cousin of the pope, who obtained permission for them to form a diocesan congregation under the jurisdiction of the local bishop. When the area of Camerino was hit hard by a plague in 1527, the little group gained great popularity due to their fearless assistance to the sick. The Duchess again interceded with Pope Clement to obtain a bull, *Religionis Zelus* (July 3, 1528), which gave definitive legal existence to these "Friars Minor of the Eremitical Life." This document allowed them to follow the Rule of Saint Francis according to "the strictest observance," to wear beards and their distinctive narrow habit with a long pointed hood, to preach to the people and to admit novices as well as other friars who might wish to transfer from the Regular Observance. They were to elect a vicar general who remained theoretically subject to the Conventual general minister.

Other friars soon joined, and the following year, 1529, the new reform held its first chapter at Albacina. It drew up a set of constitutions which prescribed a liturgy Spartan in its severity (including the celebration of Midnight Matins), two hours of meditation daily, penitential practices such as the discipline (self-flagellation) and strict dietary regulations, poor churches and houses with only a few books and itinerant preaching without remuneration. The whole aura of this legislation evokes the image of the primitive Order as depicted in the Spiritual treatise *The Mirror of Perfection*. Although the chapter elected Matteo as vicar general, he resigned within two months, to be succeeded by Ludovico of Fossombrone. As the friars began to move about preaching, people began calling them *capuccini* or "little hoods," due to the absence of a cowl on their habits; this nickname soon was adopted by the friars themselves.

Meanwhile, the new general minister of the Observants, Paolo Pisotti, was giving a difficult time to the friars who wished to form houses of recollection favored by his predecessor, Quiñones.

Although the pope himself, through his decree *In Suprema Militantis Ecclesiae* (1532), encouraged each province to found a house of rec-ollection so friars might have the opportunity to live the Rule in a stricter way, Pisotti and some other leaders continued to oppose these efforts. This led many zealous Observants, led by Bernardino of Asti (d. 1554) and Francesco of Jesi, to transfer *en masse* to the new Capuchin reform. By the chapter of 1535, it numbered some seven hundred friars, when, in reaction to Ludovico's autocratic style of leadership, Bernardino of Asti was elected vicar general.

The appeal of these new reforms cannot be viewed simply from the perspective of internal Franciscan history. They also represent an attempt to respond to dramatically changing religious and social con-ditions. For three decades, central Italy had been laid waste by marauding French and Imperial armies, leaving devastation and poverty in their wake. This fed an apocalyptic mood among the peo-ple, a sense that impending cataclysms were about to engulf Christendom. Such threats could only be met by deep repentance and reform. Indeed, in the very years Capuchins were forming, much of Italy was experiencing a sense of doom. Pope Clement had allied himself with France and Venice in an attempt to break the power of Emperor Charles V, but the forces of the emperor proved victorious and invaded central Italy. Not having been paid for months, the soldiers —mainly Germans—ransacked and pillaged the region, sacking the city of Rome itself in 1527 and making the pope a virtual prisoner. Indeed, Francisco Quiñones had spent a good deal of time serving as mediator between the pope and the emperor. But in turn, that inva-sion had been provoked by the greatest cataclysm to confront Franciscans and the rest of Europe during these years: the Protestant Reformation, which began the same year the Franciscan Order was divided. Its impact, and the ways in which the Catholic Church responded to it, refashioned the world of Franciscanism.

Like Catholics everywhere, Franciscans were divided by the call of the Reformers. When Martin Luther first mounted his challenge to church teaching in 1517, many thoughtful Christians did not know quite how to assess it. After all, the Lesser Brothers had begun as an evangelical reform movement, and many friars had instinctive sympathy with a call to reform the church according to Biblical standards. Indeed, almost all committed Catholics in the early sixteenth century recognized the need for a good deal of change in the institutional church. And for the first decade or so after Luther had issued his challenges to the established order, it seemed that with the support of Emperor Charles, pressure might be exerted on the papacy by a general church council to make reforms that would keep Luther and his followers in the church. Indeed, a friar as orthodox and zealous as the general minister, Quiñones, saw good points in Luther's initial agenda. While discussions continued, however, the rush of events in Germany forced the friars there to take sides.

For the most part, German Franciscans were early and vocal critics of the incipient Protestant Reform. One of the first and most formidable of Luther's opponents was the Conventual Franciscan, Thomas Murner (1475–1537). A doctor in both theology and law and a brilliant satirist, he at first considered Luther a kindred spirit, but by 1521, recognizing the increasingly radical nature of his attacks on Catholic doctrine and religious life, turned against him. On the other hand, the Observant Konrad Pellikan (1478–1556), a well-known humanist, gradually became drawn to the new movement. One of the first Christian scholars to gain an excellent knowledge of Hebrew as well as Greek, Pellikan was guardian of the community in Basel, where he

Konrad Pellikan, a Franciscan humanist who joined the Protestant reform.

cooperated with Erasmus in publishing editions of the writings of the
church fathers. But in 1526, he decided he could no longer profess the
Catholic faith and was invited by Zwingli to serve as professor of biblical languages in Zurich.

As the rhetoric heated up on both sides, Protestant polemicists
hurled savage insults at the Franciscans, the most famous of which
was Erasmus Alber's satirical pamphlet, *The Alkoran of the Barefoot
Friars*, a vicious parody of Bartholomew of Pisa's *Book of
Conformities*. Such attacks were meant to discredit Franciscans precisely because they were effective defenders of the traditional faith.
As rulers in various parts of Germany came to accept the
Reformation in their territories, Franciscans were banished from
their houses or forced to abandon the religious life. The two branches
of the Order lost over three hundred houses in Germany over the
next decades.

In England, once Henry VIII had definitively broken with Rome,
the religious orders were in trouble, even though in 1534 the provin-
cials of all the mendicants except the Observant Franciscans had
pledged their loyalty to the king. At the time, the Conventuals in
England numbered about 1,000, the Observants about 150. The latter had arrived in England only in 1482 and ironically had been
greatly favored by the Tudor dynasty. Two of their houses were at the
palaces of Greenwich and Richmond, where they officiated at many
religious services for the royal family. Their closeness to Queen
Catherine and strong Roman ties made them implacable opponents
of Henry's divorce. The provincial, William Peto, had in fact boldly
denounced it in a sermon in Henry's presence in 1532 and was
promptly exiled as a result. In 1534, the axe fell. The Observant communities were disbanded: friars considered intransigent were imprisoned, others fled the country and the remainders were lodged with
the Conventuals. John Forest, guardian of the community at
Greenwich and confessor to Queen Catherine, was burnt at the stake
in 1538 for refusing to submit to the royal claim of supremacy. But

the Conventuals did not survive for long; they were suppressed, along with the other religious orders, in 1538–1539. The royal inspectors found that most Franciscan houses were actually quite poor. Some friars were given paltry pensions; others accepted the new order of things and found employment as chaplains or parish priests. Henry's policy was also extended to his lordship of Ireland, but it had effect only in that part of the island under direct supervision of the crown. Since most of the Conventual houses were in this area, they bore the brunt of the secularization of the friaries. The majority of the Observant houses were in the west, and so for some years their traditional way of life continued undisturbed.

Despite these developments, the Emperor Charles and many leading "spirituals" among the Catholic intelligentsia still hoped that the papacy might yet arrive at some agreement with the Protestant Reformers to keep Western Christendom united. However, in 1541, a colloquy of leading Catholic and Protestant theologians failed to reach agreement, and intransigent forces began to dominate the curia. Conservative fears that so-called evangelical currents were spreading in the Papal States led to the establishment of a Roman Inquisition in 1542. One of those suspected of harboring such sympathies was Bernardino Ochino, vicar general of the Capuchin friars since 1538 and one of the most prominent preachers in Italy. He was cited to appear before the Inquisition in Rome; instead, he scampered over the Alps to Geneva, where he was warmly received by John Calvin. Ochino afterward led a checkered career as a Protestant controversialist, eventually dying in Moravia in 1564. His defection drew suspicion on the entire Capuchin movement, but under the able leadership of Francesco of Jesi, the new reform regained the confidence of the papacy.

By the time Pope Paul III was finally able to convoke a general council in Trent in 1545, few bishops desired to make conciliatory overtures to the Protestant Reformers. Rather, the prevailing mood was to consolidate the position of those Christians who remained loyal to the traditional faith by clearly defining the church's teaching and enacting needed reform measures. Franciscans played a notable role during the sessions of the council, which met on and off for eighteen years. The Conventual friar Cornelio Musso (1511–1574), bishop of Bitonto, a renounced orator known as the "Italian Demosthenes," was chosen to give the inaugural address opening the council sessions. He also played an important role in the formulation of the council's decree on justification, which attempted to respond to the Lutheran challenge of salvation by faith alone, as well as the decree on preaching. The latter, stating that preaching the gospel was the "principal duty" of bishops, incorporated Francis' own description of preaching, urging pastors to announce to the people, "with briefness and plainness of speech, the vices they must avoid and the virtues they must follow." Over 130 Franciscans served as advisors or *periti* at the council, insuring that its doctrinal decrees incorporated the Scotistic as well as the Thomistic position on disputed theological issues.

Saint Joseph of Cupertino, the "flying friar," as depicted in an eighteenth-century engraving.

To some extent, the decrees of Trent restricted the extensive privileges extended to friars in previous centuries, for they emphasized that public preaching was an essential element of the ordained ministry; as such, it had to be conducted under the authority of the local bishop. Furthermore, by mandating seminary training for all priests, the council finally addressed one of the major shortcomings of the medieval church: the lack of education among the clergy. As these decrees were implemented, and more and more diocesan priests began preaching regularly, the friars lost their unique position as popular preachers. Instead, Franciscans gradually focused their ministry on giving sermons for special occasions, working with confraternities—especially the Third Order—as spiritual advisors or engaging in a new evangelizing tool: the parish mission. The mission was a favored means of religious revival among Franciscans during this period. It was intended mainly for Catholics in small towns and villages who still did not have access to religious resources: educating them in the faith, renewing their devotion and leading them to lives of committed religious practice. A team of mission preachers would go out to a town for a period of several weeks or even months, employing a wide gamut of pastoral techniques during their stay: formal preaching, catechizing, hearing confessions, processions, theatrical presentations and organizing lay confraternities to carry on religious activities once the mission was over.

•   •   •

The Baroque piety that characterized Counter-Reformation Catholicism emphasized interiorizing religious feeling and hence played on elements that would heighten a personal affective response. This led to an emotional devotional piety with sometimes flamboyant expressions. Consequently, there was a great interest in mystical experience. Joseph of Cupertino (1603–1663), a Conventual friar who was often caught up in ecstasy, even episodes of levitation, aroused great popular fascination, although these also caused him much harassment by church authorities and his fellow friars. One manifestation of the spirituality of the period was concern with preparing for death. One friar constructed a vivid meditation on that reality out of the bones of four thousand of his deceased brothers and laypeople buried in the crypt of the Capuchin church in Rome.

Counter-Reformation piety, building on the Tridentine decree on justification, emphasized the role of human effort in cooperating with
God's grace. As one scholar has described it, the resulting spirituality
was one of "intensely cultivated inwardness" that emphasized ceaseless effort on the part of the individual, combating against sin to
achieve a life of Christian perfection. It is not surprising that in an age
that exalted such spiritual "heroism" the stricter forms of Franciscan
life had great appeal. In addition to the Capuchins, other new
reformed movements sprang up. The Discalced Franciscans, as mentioned at the beginning of this chapter, were a small Spanish group
enjoying great autonomy while theoretically subject to the
Conventual general. But they began to expand when, in 1541, they
received papal permission to receive any Observants seeking a "most
strict observance" who might wish to transfer. Among those who did
so was the charismatic figure of Peter of Alcantara (1499–1562), who
had been minister of the Observant Province of San Gabriel, where
he had met opposition because of his uncompromising vision of
Franciscan life. His severe practices astonished Teresa of Avila, who
often asked his guidance. "Among other austerities," she said, "he

slept only an hour and a half a night
which he took sitting down...and often
took food only once in three days.... He
was so thin that he looked like nothing
more than a knotted root...but with all
this, he was always affable." After Peter's
death, in 1563, Pius IV placed the
Discalced friars under the jurisdiction of
the Observant general, but they continued to observe their distinctive statutes
in their own provinces. They gradually
spread throughout Spain, Portugal and
their colonies, as well as in the Kingdom
of Naples.

*The monumental cemetery
in the Capuchin Church of
the Immaculate Conception,
Rome.*

In Italy, the movement for houses of recollection also gained headway once the Observant general chapter of 1535 realized the Order had to stop the hemorrhaging of its more zealous friars to the Capuchins. The friars who lived in these stricter houses became known as Reformed Friars Minor or *Riformati,* and they eventually pushed to achieve autonomy from their superiors. Recreating the tensions between the Conventuals and Observants a century earlier, the relation between "stricter" and "regular" Observant friars became quite contentious. The *Riformati* finally were granted permission to draw up their own statutes in 1582, and four years later they were organized into their own separate provinces, parallel to the existing Observant ones, although still recognizing the ultimate authority of the general minister. The friars following the Reformed Franciscan life rapidly spread throughout Italy and also achieved significant growth in central and eastern Europe: Bavaria, Poland and the lands of the Austrian Habsburgs.

In northwestern Europe also, a similar emphasis on a simpler, more contemplative life arose with a movement known as the Recollect Franciscans. Their goal was to make every friary a "house of recollection." The first communities were founded in France in the 1580s and spread widely in the early 1600s. Like their Discalced and Reformed brethren, they drew up their own statutes, eventually forming their own provinces. The Recollects were also zealous in the apostolate, providing chaplains for the French army and for many charitable institutions. The movement quickly spread to the Low Countries and Germany, although with more moderate regulations. Over the course of the seventeenth century, all of the existing provinces in that region, as

Peter of Alcantara, leader of the Discalced Reform, as depicted by Luis Tristán in Toledo, Spain.

well as the English and Irish provinces, adopted this version of the
Recollect way of life. Within only a century after their foundation,
there were almost four hundred Recollect friaries with more than five
thousand members.

Thus, by 1680, the Observant Friars Minor comprised a kaleido-
scope of distinct modes of Franciscan life: the Regular Observants
and four families of "stricter observance": the Discalced, Reformed,
French Recollects and German-Belgian Recollects. Although all
were theoretically under the leadership of one minister general, the
various stricter observances enjoyed a considerable amount of autonomy. Meanwhile, the Capuchin friars, in light of their great growth,
had achieved total independence from the Conventuals in 1619,
becoming the third independent congregation of Franciscan friars
when their superior was recognized as a general minister in his own
right. The Conventuals themselves were numerically eclipsed during
these years, becoming the smallest branch of the Franciscan Order,
since the vibrant renewal movements attracted the bulk of the vocations to Franciscan life. As a result, there were many large houses
with only a few friars; in 1652, Pope Innocent X ordered the suppression of these smaller communities, causing the Conventuals to lose
about 25 percent of their friaries in Italy. Furthermore, in the Iberian
Peninsula, the Order had actually ceased to exist, as, in 1566, the
remaining Conventuals there were incorporated into the Regular
Observants by Pope Pius V. Still, despite these reverses, the
Conventual friars continued to maintain a proud intellectual tradition, with many active in scholarship and teaching in universities.

The latter part of the sixteenth century witnessed a Europe
increasingly divided into opposing confessional blocks. A series of
reforming popes after the Council of Trent took strong moves to con-
centrate church authority even more firmly in the papal curia. One of
them was a Franciscan: a former general of the Conventuals, Felice
Peretti, who took the name Sixtus V (1585–1590). As Franciscans

committed themselves to the mission of the reinvigorated Tridentine church, they became zealous agents of a restored Catholicism and therefore logical victims of persecution where Protestant governments were in control. In the Netherlands, the northern provinces where Calvinists were in the majority struggled to gain independence from Spanish rule. Nevertheless, there remained Catholic pockets in the region. Thus, when a motley band of Protestant warriors seized the small town of Gorcum in 1572, they rounded up eleven Franciscans, headed by the local guardian, Nicholas Pieck. The friars, along with a several other priests, were brutally tortured and then hanged from the rafters of a turf shed. In France, the long wars of religion which ravaged the country from 1562 to 1598 assumed a particular savagery. In 1568, for example, in the town of Vézelay, Huguenots buried the guardian of the Franciscan community alive, with only his head remaining above the ground, using it as the target in a game in which the "bowling balls" were the severed heads of the other friars in his community. With such vicious acts of brutality on both sides, it is not surprising that there was a fusion of religious devotion and political engagement on the part of zealous Franciscans.

A striking example of this blend was the Capuchin house in Paris, founded in the early 1570s, which rapidly became a vibrant religious center favored by King Henry III. One of Henry's court favorites, or "mignons," was Henri de Joyeuse (1563–1608), a member of a prominent aristocratic family. Following the death of his young wife, he left court in 1587 to enter the Capuchins, taking the name Frère Ange, and was ordained a priest. However, following the deaths of his father and brothers in the wars against the Huguenots, the Catholics of Languedoc desperately needed an experienced commander and approached Ange to take up the task. Replying that he "would be happy to devote his blood and life for the preservation and defense of the Catholic religion," the friar petitioned Pope Clement VIII to release him from his vows to lead the resistance. However, after

Henry IV's religious settlement in 1598, Ange returned to his life as a Capuchin, becoming well-known as a preacher and spiritual director; he eventually became provincial minister of France. One of his confreres was the notable spiritual author, Benet of Canfield (1562–1610). He was born William Fitch to an Anglican family. As a young lawyer in London, he experienced a profound religious conversion, deciding in 1585 to become a Catholic. Journeying to the continent, he entered the Capuchins in Paris and served for many years as director of novices. His most famous work, *The Rule of Perfection*, distills the essence of spirituality to surrendering to the will of God, in this way appropriating the passion of Christ in one's life. This work had a great influence in seventeenth-century France. In the following decades, another Capuchin, Père Joseph (du Tremblay)—called by contemporaries the *éminence gris*—combined the career of a zealous preacher with that of confidant and military advisor to Cardinal Richelieu.

William Fitch left his homeland for France after his conversion because English Roman Catholics were in difficult straights after 1570. That year, Pope Pius V made the strategic blunder of deposing Elizabeth I, thus forcing Catholics to side with either the pope or their queen. Priests were considered traitors. Despite these hostile conditions, a second English Franciscan Province was reborn under the leadership of John Gennings (c. 1570–1660), also a convert to Catholicism, who established a friary at Douai in 1614. This was the only established friary of the new province, which served as its house of formation. The other friars lived as "underground" missionaries in England in the homes of Catholic gentry, always under the threat of exile or death, ministering to a dwindling flock of adherents.

The late 1500s also witnessed a steady expansion of English power over the Irish-speaking areas of Ireland, with the planting of English and Scottish Protestant settlers. With this came a systematic persecution of Catholic clergy; over thirty friars, including Patrick

O'Healy, bishop of Mayo, lost their lives. Nevertheless, the Irish Observant Province flourished throughout the seventeenth century, generally maintaining about four hundred members. Candidates for the Order left their homeland for the continent, where they were trained in houses of formation in Louvain, Rome and Prague, before returning home as missionaries. These colleges were also centers of scholarship in both theology and Irish culture. The most famous writer was Luke Wadding (1588–1657), the founder of St. Isidore's College in Rome. A native of Waterford, he was educated in Portugal and Spain, originally coming to Rome in 1618 to promote the cause of the definition of the doctrine of the Immaculate Conception. He spent the rest of his life there engaged in scholarship, most celebrated for his edition of the writings of John Duns Scotus and the *Annales Ordinis Minorum*, a monumental documented history of the Order.

CHAPTER EIGHT

All Peoples and Tongues

The sixteenth and seventeenth centuries represented the greatest geographical expansion of Christianity since its first centuries, and Franciscans, as the largest missionary Order of the time, played a major role in this effort. However, the fact that Spain and Portugal were the chief agents of this expansion colored it tremendously. A unique militaristic fusion of national identity and Catholic faith had formed on the Iberian peninsula over the five centuries of the *Reconquista*, and so it was natural that friars who went on mission from those countries generally carried their ethno-religious chauvinism with them. Also, these Franciscans' mission efforts were both assisted and hindered by the "royal patronage" bestowed on their monarchs by the papacy, which left the financial support and supervision of the missionaries in the hands of the crown. Finally, Franciscans of the Iberian peninsula inherited the Joachite millenarian enthusiasm that had long flourished in that region, especially in reform groups. They were convinced that they were living in the end times, so their task of bringing the gospel to newly discovered peoples took on a particular urgency.

Portugal was the first to venture out into the Atlantic, taking advantage of its geographical position to try to outflank its enemy, the Moors, and establish direct contact with interior Africa and the realms of eastern Asia. Prince Henry the Navigator (1394–1460) launched annual expeditions that inched further and further south along the African coast, discovering Madeira and the Azores, eventually establishing bases at islands closer to the coast, such as Cape Verde (1460) and São Tomé (1493). Here the raising of sugar cane became the dominant enterprise, which could only be maintained through the importation of slaves from the mainland. Church sanction of this development had been given by Nicholas V in his bull *Dum Diversas* (1452), which encouraged the Portuguese king to participate in Crusading efforts by allowing him to "invade, search out, capture and subjugate Saracens, pagans and other unbelievers...and to reduce their persons to perpetual slavery." Although a vibrant Afro-Portuguese Catholic population formed on the islands, attempts by missionaries, including Franciscans, to evangelize the peoples on the mainland were sporadic and did not extend further than a small coastal area. This was largely because the coming of Christianity implied enslavement for native peoples.

In Africa, the most sustained mission efforts were made under Capuchin friars, who arrived under the auspices of the Congregation for the Propagation of the Faith in the 1660s. In the Congo, they ministered to a people whose rulers had accepted Catholicism in the early 1500s, but where the church had never achieved a strong footing due to the failure to build up a native clergy. They also carried on an extensive ministry in neighboring Angola, where the Portuguese had established a presence. But the focus of the church's mission efforts had moved away from Africa, The widely heralded voyages of Christopher Columbus across the Atlantic in 1492 and of Vasco da Gama to India in 1498 had opened up more appealing avenues for European expansion.

Spain, or more technically, the Kingdom of Castile, which had sponsored Columbus's voyage, had also been venturing into the Atlantic, seizing the Canary Islands in the 1400s. Unlike the Portuguese islands, the Canaries were already inhabited; the natives, called Guanches, proved quite receptive to Christianity despite the oppression of their Spanish conquerors. Franciscans, among them Diego (Didacus) of Alcalá (d. 1463), provided most of the missionaries to the Canaries. They opposed the enslavement of the native peoples who accepted baptism and persuaded Pope Eugene IV to allow their ordination to the priesthood.

News of Columbus' discovery of new islands across the sea where "barbarous tribes live" who knew nothing of the Christian faith provoked enthusiastic interest at the chapter of the Ultramontane Observants in 1493; two of the volunteers managed to accompany Columbus on his second voyage later that year. They were the first of almost 8,500 Spanish Franciscans who would set out for the Americas over the next three centuries, comprising over half of all the missionaries sent by that nation to the New World. However, evangelization of the native population in the Caribbean islands did not really begin in earnest until 1500 when a larger contingent of friars arrived and began carrying out their instructions to "bring the inhabitants of the said islands to our Catholic faith." Their first report home mentioned three thousand baptisms. In 1505 these friars were organized into an independent province of the Holy Cross, with its motherhouse in Santo Domingo. From this base, expansion to the rest of the Antilles soon followed. These early missionaries were forced to work within the confines of the so-called *encomienda* system, which extended to the Americas an essentially feudal method employed in subduing recently conquered areas in Spain. Although the indigenous people technically remained in possession of their land, they were made wards of particular Spanish settlers who were given the responsibility to "protect" them and instruct them in Christianity in return for benefiting from their labor. This system rapidly became a tool of ruthless exploitation of the native peoples, who ended up as virtual slaves of the conquistadores.

A fresh opportunity presented itself, however, in the wake of the rapid conquest of the great Aztec empire by Hernándo Cortez between 1519 and 1521. Recognizing that missionaries were urgently needed for evangelizing its millions of inhabitants, Cortez appealed directly to Emperor Charles V, requesting priests who would not demand tithes and taxes, but set a good example of Christian living, specifically observant friars. Charles immediately turned to his Franciscan confessor, who in 1523 dispatched three Flemish friars to Mexico; one of them, a lay brother, Pieter van der Moere of Ghent (c. 1480–1572), enjoyed a personal relationship with the emperor as the illegitimate son of the Emperor Maximilian. He would be known in Mexico as Pedro de Gante. The following year twelve more friars arrived. They had been personally selected by the Observant general minister, Francisco Quiñones, from the strictest province in Spain, San Gabriel in Extremadura, formed by the followers of Juan de Guadalupe after the union of 1517 and were led by their former provincial, Martin of Valencia. As they trekked barefoot toward Mexico City in their shabby habits, one of them, Toribio de Benavente (d. 1568) heard natives exclaiming to one another, "*motolonía!*" Inquiring what this word meant, he was told that they were saying "poor men." He resolved that would be his name from then on.

In so doing, Toribio expressed the conviction of these "Twelve Apostles of Mexico"—strongly emphasized by Quiñones—that their primary means of evangelization would be their Franciscan witness of humility and poverty. Pope Adrian VI, through the bull *Omnimoda*, had also given them a large measure of autonomy in setting up a new local church. This led the first generation of Franciscans in Mexico to try to construct an "Indian Church" on the virgin soil of the Americas, free of the corrupting influences that had weakened European

Christianity. The methods they used to accomplish this task were ambivalent. On the one hand, they made truly heroic efforts to learn the languages of the native peoples, especially Nahuatl, the official language of the Aztec Empire, developing many tools to assist them in the task of evangelization: dictionaries, catechisms and prayer books. Pedro de Gante was especially active in this regard: He quickly opened a school in Mexico City in 1529, designed to provide an elementary education in grammar, mathematics and trades to Aztec children, and also set to work on several catechisms. In 1536, the friars opened the college of Santa Cruz de Tlatelolco in order to provide a higher education in the liberal arts and sciences to the youths from the upper echelons of Aztec society, with the hope of forming candidates for a native clergy. As time went on, the friars grew frustrated with the limitations of the *encomienda* system; they came to favor in their newer missions the methods of the *doctrina* (building churches in existing Indian villages) or the "reduction"— gathering scattered indigenous people into a compound around a friary. In both cases, the Indians were segregated in their own communities under the close supervision of the friars, where they could be more thoroughly evangelized and taught the elements of Christian civilization.

This paternalistic approach, however, also reveals the Spanish friars' totalitarian attitude that the religion of the indigenous peoples had to be totally eradicated. Aztec practices such as ritual human sacrifice and open homosexual behavior—clearly "works of the devil"— confirmed their belief that the native peoples had been corrupted because of their idolatry. Forming communities under the supervision of the friars would free them from the grip of their pagan past. Nevertheless, despite the consequent destruction of much of native culture, the friars preserved other elements—especially chants and dances—which they believed could be reconciled with Christian life. We owe much of our knowledge of Aztec culture to the work of friars, such as Toribio de Motolinía's *History of New Spain,* Jerónimo de Mendieta's *History of the Indian Church,* and the *General History of the Things of New Spain* of Bernardino de Sahagún (1499–1590), a veritable encyclopedia of Aztec culture composed in Nahuatl.

Other Franciscans, especially in later decades, were not as favorable toward the native peoples. For example, Diego de Landa, provincial of the Yucatan, was particularly severe in uprooting native religion, launching in 1562 a local inquisition that brought brutal torture to the Mayans. Such attitudes reflected the growing European influence in Mexico. As more Spaniards settled in the country, they wanted to order society and church on a European model. The royal government was also reluctant to empower the indigenous population, leading the First Council of Mexico in 1555 to forbid the ordination of natives to the priesthood. The millennial hopes of the first Franciscans faded in light of new realities.

Meanwhile, Spanish conquistadores were also overcoming the peoples of South America, most importantly through the conquest of the vast Inca Empire between 1526 and 1540. Missionaries tended

Pedro de Gante (c. 1480–1572) dedicated his ministry to educating Mexican youth for half a century. He was beatified by John Paul II in 1988.

to employ the methods they had developed in Mexico, but their task was made much more difficult because of the turbulence of the conquest, which involved civil war among the Spaniards and rebellion by the natives. Franciscans first established themselves in Quito in 1537 and then in Lima in 1545. By mid-century they were building residences in Indian villages. They also eventually began to penetrate Chile, Bolivia and the La Plata region. Here the humble Francisco Solano (1549–1610) was one of the great figures in the Spanish missionary efforts. He came to America in 1589, laboring in the region of Tucumán (present-day southern Bolivia and northern Argentina), becoming noted for his facility in learning native languages and using music as a tool of evangelization.

Franciscans were also active on the northern frontiers of the Spanish empire, in what is now the United States. They arrived in Florida in 1573, eight years after the first permanent Spanish settlement in St. Augustine, but a sustained mission effort did not begin until larger contingents of friars arrived near the end of the century. Since the tribes in northern Florida were town-dwellers, they established themselves in these existing villages. At their height in 1675, forty friars were maintaining some thirty-six mission stations. But Florida soon fell victim to the expanding presence of the English colonies to the north. A series of slave-taking raids by English soldiers and their Native American allies essentially wiped out these missions by 1706.

In the west, Franciscans accompanied the Spanish colonizing expeditions that reached New Mexico in 1598 and quickly began evangelizing the Pueblo peoples in the region. By 1630 the friars had established missions in some twenty-five pueblos, baptizing most of the fifty thousand natives. This work was interrupted by the great Pueblo Revolt of 1680, which put a temporary end to the New Mexico colony: The Spanish settlers were expelled, and twenty-three friars were killed. The missions were reestablished only after the Spanish reoccupied the territory in 1692.

To the north, the French had entered the race for colonies

Missionary Saint Francisco Solano in South America.

in America with a settlement at Quebec in 1608, but the small colony was without clergy until Champlain invited the Recollect Franciscans to come in 1615. In addition to serving as chaplains to the Quebec garrison, they undertook missions to the Montagnais and Huron peoples. However, the Recollects were driven from Canada in 1629 when the English briefly seized the colony and did not return to New France until 1670. They founded three friaries—at Quebec, Trois-Rivières and Montreal—also resuming their missionary activities among the native peoples and serving as chaplains to exploratory expeditions and in military posts in the Great Lakes region. Notable among these friars was Louis Hennepin, the first European to visit Niagara Falls, who later penned colorful accounts of his journeys. Meanwhile, the French government assigned the territory of Acadia to the Capuchins in 1632, where they labored among the Penobscot people until 1654, when the British captured the French settlements there. However, in 1720, Capuchins arrived in Louisiana, where they were given responsibility for the French settlers and the native peoples along the Mississippi south of the Ohio River. A few English

Franciscans were active in Maryland, a fact that has often escaped notice. Due to the small number of Jesuits available for the colony, the proprietor, Lord Baltimore, called for assistance. In response, the English Recollect province sent two missionaries to work in southern Maryland in 1672, where they maintained a presence until 1718.

Louis Hennepin, a French Recollect missionary, published in Europe several accounts (which were prone to exaggeration) of his travels in America.

In the Portuguese colony of Brazil, the Jesuits were the only organized Catholic missionary presence until some Franciscans arrived in the 1580s and began working at Olinda in the northeast part of the country. However, their evangelizing efforts to the natives were continually stymied by the

Portuguese settlers. The thriving local economy was based almost entirely on sugar plantations, so colonists were constantly attempting to seize Indians as slaves. In addition, African slaves were being imported to Brazil in very high numbers—perhaps 3.5 million people over three centuries—to replace those being worked to death in the sugar plantations.

It was Capuchin Franciscans who mounted the first sustained critique of the slave trade; perhaps the fact that they worked under the auspices of the Propagation of the Faith, rather than under royal patronage, gave them a certain freedom in this regard. In the 1680s, two friars in Havana, Francisco de Jaca and Epifanio Moirans, witnessing the plight of slaves there, began preaching that landowners should, in justice, free them. They were promptly arrested as a result; rather than repenting of their attitude, Epifanio wrote a treatise condemning the entire institution of slavery. He was then excommunicated by the archbishop and shipped back to Europe. However, his outcry coupled with the growing complaints of his Capuchin confreres laboring in Angola, where entire communities were being ravaged by the drive to round up slaves. These protests caused the Capuchin general curia in 1684 to make a formal protestation to the Congregation of the Propagation of the Faith, which ruled that the existing slave trade was indeed immoral, a decision upheld by the Holy Office in 1686. This decision of the church had virtually no effect, however, in light of the entrenched economic and political interests that benefited from the existing system.

In India, the Portuguese conquered the territory around Goa in 1510; the Franciscans, who established themselves in 1517, were the major force in the evangelization of the native population in the surrounding regions until the arrival of the Jesuits later in the century The first bishop of Goa was a Franciscan, João of Albuquerque (1537–1553), who established a college for the purpose of training a native clergy. Conversions, however, progressed slowly and were limited almost exclusively to lower caste Indians. The most spectacular success was the conversion of the Paravas, a fishing people on the Coromandel coast, among whom Saint Francis Xavier later labored with great effect. Franciscans were also missionaries in Sri Lanka beginning in the early seventeenth century.

The Spanish established their own Asian base with their occupation of the Philippines in 1569. Augustinian friars arrived in the islands in 1575, but Discalced Franciscans soon followed them in 1578. Interestingly enough, these Spanish friars came to the Philippines across the Pacific Ocean, as an extension of their presence in New Spain. The friar missionaries, sensing the fundamental openness of the natives, attempted to avoid many of the abuses that marred evangelization efforts in America. Rather, they enticed native chieftains to gather the scattered population in reductions "to bring them to civilization and Christianization." Convinced that "the needs of the body are just as urgent and important as the needs of the soul," the friars founded schools and hospitals and brought improvements in agriculture: the use of irrigation, cattle and plows. As in Mexico, Franciscans emphasized the need to learn native languages and evangelize by means of them. By the early 1580s, Juan de Plasencia had compiled a Tagalog grammar, dictionary and catechism.

From the Philippines, Franciscans went to Japan and China. Catholic missions in Japan had been dominated by the Jesuits since the arrival of Francis Xavier in 1549. Subsequently, the Jesuits had developed a strategy of missionary enculturation, conforming themselves to Japanese patterns of diet, clothing and etiquette in an attempt to win over the feudal nobility of the country. During these years, the Portuguese had held a commercial monopoly in Japan, but the Spanish, once based in the Philippines, also began to seek entry. In 1593, Franciscans arrived, led by Pedro Bautista Blasquez, former provincial of the Philippines. They settled in Kyoto, where they built a church and a hospital. Other friars arrived the following year, enabling them to found houses at Osaka and Nagasaki. Their missionary approach focused on the poor and outcast, such as beggars and lepers, providing a marked contrast with that of the Jesuits, who attempted to work from the upper class downward. However, mounting Japanese fears of Spanish conquest brought a harsh response from the regent Hideyoshi, who ordered the arrest of the Spanish missionaries. In February, 1597, twenty-six Christians were crucified at Nagasaki, including Pedro Bautista and five other friars, along with three Japanese Jesuits and seventeen Japanese laymen, most of whom were members of the Franciscan Third Order. With a change in government the next year, however, other Franciscans quickly returned to Japan. Christianity enjoyed great success in Japan over the next two decades with perhaps three hundred thousand converts, but foreign missionaries were banished in 1614 and a wave of severe persecutions followed in which thousands of Christians lost their lives, driving the few remaining Christians in the country underground.

The ultimate goal of Catholic missionaries in Asia was the great empire of China, which under the Ming dynasty had remained closed to foreigners. The Portuguese had managed to establish a small enclave for commercial purposes in Macao in 1554, however, and from this base missionaries attempted to penetrate the mainland. Finally, in 1583, Jesuits got permission to reside in the country. Under the leadership of Matteo Ricci, they pursued the same methods of cultural assimilation pioneered in Japan. Some decades later, Spanish friars, both Franciscan and Dominican, also gained access to the country. They rejected the Jesuit methods as making too many accommodations to false religions; rather they emphasized direct proclamation of the gospel. They

Memorial to the twenty-six martyrs of Nagasaki.

also believed that the gospel demanded greater attention to the needs of the poor, even if this meant risking the anger of local authorities. This sparked the famous "Chinese rites" controversies, which raged both in China and in Rome for a century, until the Jesuit accommodations were finally condemned by the Vatican in 1742.

The Conventual Franciscans, largely excluded from this vast work of evangelization to the Americas, Asia and Africa, developed their own field of missionary endeavor in eastern Europe—especially Moldavia, Wallachia and Bulgaria—under the auspices of the Congregation for the Propagation of the Faith, where they ministered to small, scattered groups of Catholics. There they built churches and schools and printed Moldavian and Romanian grammars and catechetical materials. They also worked on negotiations for reunion of various Eastern churches with Rome.

By the early eighteenth century, Franciscan missionary efforts had largely stabilized. However, several new fields did open, two of them on the northern frontier of Mexico. Threatened by the expansion of other European powers into the regions of Texas and California, the Spanish crown determined to use the traditional method of military posts and the Christianization of the native inhabitants to secure them. In the early 1700s, Franciscans established

themselves in Texas under the leadership of Antonio Margil. Despite the zealous efforts of the friars, these missions were never very successful in numerical terms as their highly structured life was unattractive to the nomadic native peoples.

The last major area of evangelization in this period was opened up by the expulsion of the Jesuits from Mexico in 1767. As a result, Franciscans inherited their missions in what is now Arizona and northern Baja California. Thus they were called upon by the govern-

Junipero Serra (1713–1784), founder of the California missions. He was beatified in 1988.

ment to make a new initiative to secure Upper California. This expedition was led by Junipero Serra (1713–1784), who founded a mission at San Diego in 1769. Ultimately eighteen missions were founded by Serra himself and his successor, Fermin Lasuén (d. 1803); three more followed in the early nineteenth century. Although the California missions proved to be large, successful complexes, they were a dying breed. The friars found themselves constantly struggling with government agents who were operating out of a new "enlightened" mentality. These forces would soon close down the California missions and pose the greatest challenge to the Friars Minor in their history.

CHAPTER NINE

Tribulations and Dreams

o judge by most external criteria, Franciscans in the first half of the eighteenth century were flourishing. The typical ministerial activities of the friars since the Counter-Reformation period continued to attract a widespread audience. For example, Leonard of Port Maurice (1676–1751) enjoyed tremendous success as a preacher of parish missions throughout central and southern Italy; many times he was obliged to preach in the open air, as churches were not large enough to hold the crowds who came to hear him. And the Franciscan way of life continued to hold great appeal for many middle- and working-class young men: Vocations were literally pouring in. The three congregations of Friars Minor reached their all-time height in membership during these years. By 1750, there were almost

Leonard of Port Maurice (d. 1751). One of the most prominent preachers of the eighteenth century, he propagated devotion to the Stations of the Cross throughout Italy. Canonized in 1867, he is the patron of parish missions.

77,000 Observant Friars Minor, about 40,000 of which followed the Regular Observance; the rest belonged to the various families of "stricter observance": the Reformed, Recollect and Discalced Franciscans. In addition, the Capuchins had about 33,000 members and the Conventuals over 20,000. Franciscans were heavily concentrated in southern Europe: There were about 26,000 Observants and 15,000 Capuchins in Italy alone—this at a time when the peninsula held about fifteen million inhabitants. There were another 23,000 Observants in Spain and its colonies.

Unfortunately, these huge numbers—replicated to a lesser degree in other religious orders—had repercussions on internal discipline. Franciscan leaders expressed concerns about inadequate scrutiny of new candidates; furthermore, overpopulated friaries fostered idleness, creating resentment among the people asked to support them. Already in the late 1600s the Vatican attempted unsuccessfully to place a limit on the number of novices that orders could admit. But civil governments also began expressing concern about the large numbers of religious, especially as Enlightenment attitudes began to spread. The scientific revolution, especially new developments in physics and astronomy, was giving rise to the belief that the only objectively true knowledge about the world was that obtained through scientific, empirical reason. This, in turn, led to the modern myth of progress: that by means of natural reason, humanity could confidently comprehend and control the world for its advancement and perfection. Among European intellectual elites, an Enlightenment "project" emerged of creating a new, rational social order that would insure the material and moral welfare of humanity in place of the existing, repressive order imposed by pre-Enlightenment society, dominated by myths and traditions. To some radical thinkers, orthodox Christianity itself, with its irrational dogmas and superstitious devotions, was a bar to progress. From this perspective, Franciscans appeared to be vestiges of the dark medieval past; in a world focused on material progress, they seemed unproductive slackers. The French philosopher Voltaire (1694–1778) summed up such attitudes when he characterized Saint Francis as "a raving lunatic who goes about half naked, talks to animals, catechizes a wolf, and makes himself a snow wife...and whose sons, those robust lazybones, take a vow to live at our expense." In the Italian language, a word was even coined—*fratesca* ("friarish")—to describe backward attitudes and practices.

As such "enlightened" sentiments began to pervade government bureaucracies, they provided justification for monarchs determined to control the church within their domains. Most contemporary rulers were convinced that they had a right to order their nation's affairs, including its religious institutions and practices, free of interference by outsiders. The papacy became increasingly marginalized politically throughout the eighteenth century. International religious orders of men like the Franciscans stood out as symbols of resented papal centralization as well as defenders of an outdated intellectual order. The most prominent casualties of this mentality were the Jesuits. Wishing to destroy their influence in Brazil, Portugal expelled them from its domains in 1759, an action followed in the next few years by France and Spain. Finally, Pope Clement XIV (1769–1774), the Conventual Franciscan Lorenzo Ganganelli, was pressured by these powerful Catholic nations to suppress the Society in 1773. But Franciscans also became victims of politics.

Pope Clement XIV. Franciscan Lorenzo Ganganelli was a good friar and cultivated man whose temperament did not equip him for the political challenges confronting his papacy.

The French government set up a "Commission on Regulars" in 1765 under the liberal Archbishop Loménie de Brienne to examine the state of the religious orders. Three years later, the commission issued its verdict: It raised the age of entry to twenty-one, established a quota that limited the number of novices that could enter each year, closed all religious houses with fewer than nine members and prohibited orders from having more than one house in each city. Although the commission judged the Capuchins and the Recollects to be in generally good condition, it saw no real difference between the friars of the Regular Observance and the Conventuals, and so forced the former—who were much larger—to join the latter. Over the next twenty-five years, these measures fully halved the number of Franciscans in the country.

Franciscan Eulogius Schneider (1756-1794), was a gifted orator and theologian. Caught up in the fervor of the French Revolution, he left the Order and moved to Strasbourg, eventually abandoning the priesthood and becoming a leader of the left-wing Revolutionaries in the city. However, he himself became a victim of the Reign of Terror and was guillotined in 1794.

Similar restrictive measures soon followed in Spain, Portugal and various Italian states. In the 1780s, Enlightenment attitudes influenced Emperor Joseph II to implement a program of church "reform" throughout the vast domains of the Austrian Hapsburgs. In 1781, all religious houses not involved in providing some tangible benefit to society (teaching, nursing, scholarship) were suppressed and their property confiscated. Many Franciscans in central Europe took up the ministry of educating lay students during these years, in response both to the threat of suppression and to the invitation of municipalities seeking to staff colleges formerly conducted by the Jesuits.

But the slow strangulation imposed by these government actions was nothing to compare to the ferocity unleashed by the French Revolution. On February 13, 1790, the Constituent Assembly ordered the total suppression of all religious orders. Franciscans were thus "exclaustrated"—forced out of their houses, which were confiscated by the government, to fend for themselves. In 1791, they were asked to take an oath to accept the new schismatic French national church or otherwise be viewed as enemies of the Revolution. In this climate, many friars accepted the government pensions offered them. A few, like the scholar Eulogius Schneider, enthusiastically shared Revolutionary ideals. But others, loyal to the pope and their way of life, either emigrated or were deported. Several hundred Franciscans were executed in the Reign of Terror of 1793–1794.

As the Revolutionary armies proved victorious over their enemies and advanced into other countries, the wave of suppression reached into Belgium (1796), northern Italy (1802) and the Rhineland (1803). Naturally, the French puppet kingdoms of Spain and Naples adopted similar policies; finally, religious houses were suppressed in all of Italy, including even Rome itself, in 1810. Many artistic and cultural treasures of friaries ended up in municipal libraries or museums. During these years, some Franciscans in these occupied countries became virtual guerillas, inciting people to revolt against the invading French and restore traditional religious practice.

Franciso Goya's The Third of May 1808, *depicts the execution of members of the Spanish resistance by French armies. A Franciscan, to the left of the central figure, is one of the victims (Museo del Prado, Madrid).*

After Napoleon's defeat, the European powers gathered at the Congress of Vienna in 1815 with the agenda of restoring the pre-Revolutionary political order in Europe as much as possible. The ravaged Franciscan provinces in Italy, Spain and Germany were thus able to begin rebuilding. In light of their experience of the Revolution, it was natural that most Franciscans viewed its proclaimed ideals of "liberty, equality, and fraternity" as inimical to Catholicism; they were thus in total sympathy with Pope Gregory XVI's 1832 encyclical, *Mirari Vos*, which condemned the liberal values of freedom of speech and of the press, religious liberty and representative democracy.

However, because the papacy had so allied itself with conservative monarchical governments, when liberals in Catholic countries were able to gain power, it was natural for them to turn on the religious orders. This occurred in both Portugal and Spain, where all Franciscan houses were secularized in the 1830s; within a few years, hardly one remained open. Similar policies were taken by the newly independent countries of Latin America. And in Italy, a liberal nationalist movement, the *Risorgimento*, began to arise, centered in the Kingdom of Sardinia in the Piedmont region; in 1855, religious orders there were suppressed. When the forces for Italian unification succeeded in establishing the new Kingdom of Italy, these laws were extended throughout the country in 1866. Within a few years, the great friary of Aracoeli in Rome was seized by the Italian government to make room for a monument to King Victor Emmanuel II. In several non-Catholic countries, Franciscans suffered because of nationalistic attitudes. The new German empire, as part of its *Kulturkampf*—the struggle for German culture—intended to subject the Catholic church to state control, banished all religious orders from Prussian territory in 1875. The Russian government also suppressed Franciscan houses in Poland, which they viewed as vehicles of incipient Polish nationalism.

As a result, by the 1880s, Franciscans were but a fraction of their former numbers. The Observant family of the Order now numbered only 14,500 friars, the Capuchins 7,600, and the Conventuals just 1,500. This was an overall decrease of 80 percent from a century earlier.

But the problems Franciscans faced were not simply external ones. When and where they were able to start rebuilding their lives amidst the waves of suppression, exclaustrated friars brought back many of the attitudes and habits they had picked up during their years "out in the world." The reimposition of encrusted disciplines of traditional religious life seemed confining to many. As early as 1827, the Observant General minister complained about friars' abandoning Franciscan practices of poverty and prayer through their free use of money, love of secular attire and frequenting public cafes and the homes of the laity. This experience of exclaustration was not totally negative, however; friars also came to understand from their own experience many of the problems that working people were facing in a rapidly industrializing Europe as well as some of the authentic values of liberalism. Still, the general response of the church and the Order's leadership was one of opposition to modern trends. As Pius IX reminded faithful Catholics, the world was caught up in a "battle between light and darkness, truth and error, vice and virtue, Belial and Christ." In 1846, he established a new Vatican Congregation to oversee religious orders and animate their reform. In this spirit of restoration, the leaders of the various branches of the Franciscan Order emphasized the reestablishment of traditional practices of prayer and penance, the wearing of the habit and the discipline of the cloister with its "separation from the world." The Vatican Congregation for Religious took a major step in assuring higher standards when in 1857 it required that all religious orders institute a period of temporary vows before a member made solemn (permanent) profession; this provided a much greater opportunity to assess a candidate's fitness for religious life. Prior to this, Franciscans had professed final vows immediately upon completing novitiate.

Ironically, in the midst of these traumas, Franciscans were experiencing solid growth in countries that championed the very democratic liberties that the church officially condemned. Once revolutionary anticlerical fervor died down in France by the 1820s, the country experienced a great resurgence of popular religious devotion. The Capuchins were able to reestablish themselves in Provence in the 1820s, a novitiate was opened in 1837 in Lyons and in 1844 a French province was once again established. The Observants, after an absence of more than half a century, were able to establish a friary in 1849; other foundations followed quickly, and a French province was again established in 1860. In the 1870s, the newly revived Observants were approached by several bishops in French-speaking Canada to return there, in particular to minister to Third Order Franciscans. The Recollect friars who had labored in Canada during the colonial era had long disappeared, as when the British conquered Québec in 1759 they restricted the reception of novices. Frédéric Janssoone (1838–1916), a native of French Flanders, came to Canada in 1881, originally to raise funds for the friars' work in the Holy Land. He returned to stay in 1888, and a Franciscan community was founded in Montreal in 1890.

In the British Isles, liberal reform forces had enacted a Catholic Relief Act in 1791, which granted Catholics the right to worship publicly; a second act followed in 1829 that removed almost all the remaining disabilities against them. The possibilities created by these laws were too late to save the English Recollect province, however, which had been slowly declining in membership throughout the eighteenth century. The loss of its formation house in Douai during the French Revolution proved catastrophic; by 1813, there were only twenty-one friars. The final chapter of the province, with nine surviving friars, was held in 1838 and the province itself was dissolved in 1841. Eventually, the remaining elderly friars made contact with the thriving Flemish Recollect province, which was reestablished only in

1842. Bernard van Loo came to England to investigate, and soon Flemish friars began ministering in England, eventually founding houses in Sclerder, Cornwall in 1858 and at West Gorton, near Manchester, in 1861. Both the Catholic religious revival of the Oxford movement and an influx of Irish immigrants led to a growth in native vocations, and the English Recollects were reestablished as a province in 1891. The Capuchins also came to Britain at this time through the work of Louis of Lavagna, who arrived in England in 1850 en route to America, but was persuaded to stay to minister to the needs of the Catholic population in the Peckham district of London. An aristocratic convert, Lord Fielding, also invited the Capuchins to establish a house on his estate in Pantasaph, Wales in 1852. The new community quickly took root, and an English Capuchin province was formed in 1873.

The Catholic Relief Acts also affected the Irish Observants. As government persecution of religious had eased in the 1700s, most of them were able to form small communities of two or three men, many in the towns where their old friaries had been located. The friars generally cared for parishes, living and dressing more or less as diocesan priests, each managing his own finances. Candidates for the Order were admitted to an informal novitiate in various places in Ireland and then sent to one of the colleges abroad to study—their only experience of organized community life. The first Relief Act allowed the foundation of a diocesan seminary at Maynooth in 1795. As this institution prospered, large numbers of diocesan priests were now available to take charge of parishes, thus supplanting the Franciscans in that ministry. At the same time, the suppression of religious houses on the continent by Emperor Joseph II deprived them of their colleges in Prague and Louvain; even St. Isidore's in Rome was closed for some years. The friars, steadily diminishing in number, turned increasingly to the work of educating youth and also went abroad for missionary work.

By the 1850s, both Archbishop Cullen of Dublin and the General Minister Venanzio of Celano became deeply concerned about restoring "regular observance" within the Irish Province. Bernard van Loo of the Flemish province, who was already familiar with the situation in England, was appointed "visitor and reformer" in 1857. He urged the Irish friars to come together in larger houses where a common life could be established and brought over Flemish friars to establish a house in Killarney to be a "leaven" of regular observance in the country. Finally, when St. Isidore's College was taken over by Recollect reformers in the 1880s, it began producing friars trained in their model of a disciplined religious life; these men gradually replaced the old "black friars" (so called because they wore black clerical garb rather than habits) in the Irish friaries. The Irish Capuchins also began experiencing a revival in these years; they had founded a mission in 1608, which had developed into a province, but also suffered a marked decline in the eighteenth century. By the 1850s, the Order was able to begin rebuilding, so that a province was again established in 1885.

Irish Capuchin Theobald Mathew (1790–1856), was one of the leaders of the temperance movement. Several million people "took the pledge" of abstinence from alcoholic beverages under his influence.

The Irish Observants had opened their first foreign mission in Newfoundland in the 1780s. A large percentage of the inhabitants of that colony were Irish Catholics; in response to their entreaties, the British government allowed James O'Donnell, former minister of the Irish province, to minister there. Soon several other friars arrived, and O'Donnell was ordained bishop in 1796. Four other Franciscans succeeded him in that office; Michael Fleming began construction of the cathedral in St. John's, and Thomas Mullock founded a seminary, which led to the growth of a native clergy, thus eliminating the need for friar missionaries. The last of them left Newfoundland in 1877.

However, a more extensive mission field opened up for the Irish Franciscans in Australia. As the new colony began to expand, there were urgent requests for priests to minister to the Catholic population. A number of Irish friars responded to this call, beginning with Bonaventure Geoghegan, who came to Melbourne in 1839 as parish priest for what is now the entire state of Victoria; he eventually was named Bishop of Adelaide. Other Franciscans followed, all of whom labored as individual missionaries. Peter O'Farrell went to Sydney in 1854; over the years he campaigned vigorously for the foundation of a permanent Franciscan community; however, it was only after his death that three friars arrived in 1879, putting down roots among poor Irish immigrants in Waverley, outside Sydney.`

However, it was the United States of America that opened up the largest field of expansion for Franciscans in the nineteenth century. In 1830 the new nation was overwhelmingly Protestant, mostly British-Americans by ancestry or slaves of African descent; even after the incorporation of French Louisiana, there were still only about 250,000 Catholics in a nation of 13 million—about 2 percent of the population. This picture began to change, however, as 600,000 new Catholic immigrants arrived in the 1830s. Then, from 1840 to 1860, a virtual tidal wave of 3.3 million new arrivals inundated the United States, the majority of which were Irish and Germans. A good many of these immigrants—most of the Irish and a third of the Germans— were Catholics. As a result, by the outbreak of the Civil War the Roman Catholic community was transformed into the largest single religious denomination in the country (with some 3 million members, comprising 10 percent of the population). The need for clergy to minister to this population was critical.

Just as this immigration was beginning, the old Franciscan missions of the colonial epoch were rapidly becoming extinct. One or two friars still labored in New Mexico; the California missions had been confiscated by the Mexican government in the 1830s and sold off to wealthy landowners; only a handful of friars managed to hold out at Mission Santa Barbara. Although there had been a few "freelance" Observant and Capuchin friars who had come to the new United States from Ireland and the continent to work as missionaries in the late eighteenth and early nineteenth centuries, all of them labored as isolated individuals. It was only with the waves of immigrants who began arriving in the 1830s that Franciscans were able to again establish a solid footing in the country.

The first new foundation was made by Reformed Franciscans in Cincinnati. In 1838 Bishop John B. Purcell had made an extensive tour of Europe, seeking priests for his burgeoning German-speaking flock. A Bavarian friar, Francis Huber, responded; despite repeated appeals for help, his own province was unable to supply additional friars, and so Bishop Purcell turned to the Tyrolese province. William Unterthiner arrived in Cincinnati in 1844, soon followed by other friars, who spread out to care for German-speaking parishes in the region. Within a few years they established a classical college that could educate local candidates for the Order, and so the Cincinnati friars were organized in 1859 into the independent custody of St. John the Baptist, with the right to receive novices. Reformed friars also began arriving in the eastern United States. In 1854, Bishop John Timon of Buffalo, New York, approached the general minister, Venanzio of Celano, for missionaries to work in his rapidly expanding diocese. Several Italian friars volunteered, led by Panfilo da Magliano of the Abruzzi province, arriving in western New York in 1855. In 1858, they established themselves in the village of Allegany, where they founded St. Bonaventure's College and Seminary (later university). They too were organized into an independent custody, dedicated to the Immaculate Conception, in 1861. Shortly thereafter, they extended their efforts to New York City, Connecticut and

Massachusetts.

German Recollect friars came to the Midwest when Bishop Henry Juncker of Alton, Illinois, appealed to the province of Saxony for priests. The young provincial, Gregor Janknecht, assigned eight friars to this new mission. In 1858 they settled at the village of Teutopolis, Illinois, from where they went out to minister throughout farming communities in the region. The following year they assumed care of a parish in Quincy, Illinois, where in 1860 they also established a college. They soon expanded their ministry to German immigrant parishes in Missouri, Ohio and Tennessee. This foundation received a massive influx in membership in 1875 when the friars of the mother province in Saxony were forced to leave their homeland due to the *Kulturkampf*; over one hundred of them came to the United States, enabling the formation of an independent unit, Sacred Heart Province, in 1879. The *Kulturkampf* was also the occasion for another foundation of German Recollects in the United States, when friars of the small province of Thuringia came in 1875 seeking refuge, settling first in the remote diocese of Ogdensburg, New York, and then, more advantageously, in the factory city of Paterson, New Jersey.

Meanwhile, Conventual Franciscans had arrived in the country in 1852, at the request of Bishop Odin of Galveston, Texas, to care for German and Polish immigrant settlements in the state. The region was poor, and the friars, led by Leopold Moczygemba, transferred their headquarters in 1859 to Syracuse, New York, where they began ministering to German immigrant parishes in the area and established a novitiate. This American foundation was made an independent province in 1872, with Bonaventure Keller as the first minister.

The Capuchins also established a formal institutional presence in the United States during these years. Interestingly enough, this did not come about through the initiative of the Order or at the request of an American bishop, but through two young Swiss diocesan priests who dreamed of becoming missionaries to the United States and implanting the Capuchin Order there. Shortly after their arrival in the country in 1856, they met with Bishop John Martin Henni of Milwaukee, who permitted them to make a foundation at Mount Calvary, Wisconsin. A Swiss friar was sent to guide them through the novitiate, and in 1857, the two, Johann (Bonaventure) Frey and Gregor (Francis) Haas, were received into the Capuchin Order. Within twenty-five years, their community had spread to several other locations in the Midwest, and to New York and New Jersey as well, so that it became the province of St. Joseph in 1882. That same year, the Capuchins also established the province of St. Augustine, based in Pittsburgh, Pennsylvania. This community traced its origins to German friars banished from their homeland in the 1870s because of the *Kulturkampf*. Besides the Pittsburgh area, these friars had also settled in Maryland and Kansas.

For these German and Italian Franciscans, their early foundations in the United States involved a marked break from their European past. Their chief activities in America, determined by the needs of immigrant populations and the requests of bishops, were staffing parishes and conducting schools. The friars in Europe certainly had long experience with numerous pastoral ministries, especially preaching, but they very rarely had been assigned the full care of souls—with all of its administrative responsibilities—in a parochial setting. Again, Franciscans could certainly boast of a proud educational tradition, but its schools in Europe, except for Germany, were largely internal, devoted to the training of young friars. In both cases, friars were not used to handling practical matters of finance and administration. These ministerial activities also brought far-reaching changes in Franciscan life. To meet the challenges of their American missions, most friars had to seek dispensations from the Rule and the constitutions of their Orders: to wear secular clothing at times, to commute the choral celebration of the Divine Office to private recitation or even saying other prayers in its place, and—for Observants and Capuchins—to handle money and to own property in accord with American civil law. Above all, they were forced out of their cloisters into a much closer interaction with laypeople than any of them were accustomed. It was a constant struggle to establish rigorous daily structures of religious life, especially in smaller parishes. Friars facing the demands of an active ministry often viewed these traditional structures as impediments to their work. These were but a taste of the challenges that all Franciscans would face in the new century.

CHAPTER TEN

Rediscovering a Charism

As Franciscans approached the seventh centenary of their founding in 1909, they were well on the road to recovery from the traumas of the preceding century and a half. Provinces were in the process of rebuilding all over Europe. In Spain, the Observants and Capuchins, who had both been facing extinction, were allowed to reopen friaries in the late 1870s. By the end of the next decade, the worst of anticlerical legislation had been lifted in Germany and Italy as well, and Franciscans in other European countries were also experiencing solid growth. There also were encouraging signs of rebirth in Latin America. And by the early 1900s, Franciscans had vigorously renewed their commitment to Catholic world mission efforts.

This material recovery took place in the wake of a profound devotional transformation within European Catholicism. The Romantic idealization of the Middle Ages that was a feature of many of the artistic movements of the nineteenth century led to a revived interest in ritual and mystery. Certainly, the central rituals of Catholicism remained the Mass and the other sacraments, especially frequent confession, but the clergy also promoted adoration of the reserved Eucharist through frequent ceremonies of Benediction of the Blessed Sacrament. The cults of the Sacred Heart of Jesus and the Virgin Mary blossomed, as Pius IX extended the feast of the Sacred Heart to the universal church and solemnly defined the doctrine of the Immaculate Conception. There were countless new novenas, litanies and confraternities. Many of these devotions emphasized the sinfulness of fallen human nature, thus serving to fortify a "ghetto Catholicism" that wished to separate itself from the godless culture of the modern world. Most Franciscans enthusiastically promoted these devotions among the people they served and incorporated them into their own community schedules, such as daily recitation of the Franciscan crown or rosary.

This spirituality also enhanced the authority of the clergy and the institutional church which provided access to God. In a special way, popular piety was devoted to the person of the pope himself as a living icon, the earthly representative of Christ. The dominant ultramontanist theology of the period, intent on creating an authoritarian law-and-order Catholicism in the face of the challenges of a hostile world, culminated in the First Vatican Council (1869–1870) with its definition of papal infallibility. A highly centralized system of church government reached its heights in the period between 1870 and 1960.

All of these currents were evident as Franciscans went about rebuilding their lives. Like the church at large, Franciscans were intent on pursuing an agenda of restoration. Yes, friars might make some adjustments, such as using modern techniques of communication to propagate their message, but the main emphasis was on maintaining and reinforcing traditional patterns of religious life. This agenda was summarized by the Capuchin general minister, Bernard of Andermatt (1884–1908): "To keep the Seraphic Rule in all its integrity and purity, together with the commands of our constitutions and the wise traditions and customs handed down by our fathers, but taking care at the same time by prudent adaptation to mold our discipline to the conditions of the modern world."

His contemporary, the energetic Observant General Minister, Bernardino of Portogruaro (1869–1889) had blazed the way in such efforts. In an attempt to foster unity among the friars worldwide, especially where they were dispersed due to suppression of their houses, he instituted the *Acta Ordinis Minorum* in 1882 as a means of disseminating important documents from the Vatican and the Order. He also encouraged the work of friars with the many new communities of women religious following the Franciscan Third Order Regular Rule which were springing up to meet the needs of modern society, in particular education and health care. One of the most fruitful of these efforts was his own close collaboration with Mother Mary of the Passion (Hélène de Chappotin, 1839–1904), foundress of the Franciscan Missionaries of Mary, which would emerge as the largest community of Third Order women.

Bernardino was also deeply committed to reviving the Franciscan intellectual heritage, founding in 1879 the research college of San Bonaventura at Quaracchi, outside Florence, for that purpose. Its first major project was a critical edition of the works of Saint Bonaventure, thus contributing to the revival of neo-Scholastic thought which the papacy viewed as the best means of synthesizing faith and reason. All three branches of the Order established general houses of study in Rome: the Conventuals were the first, reviving their Seraphic College of St. Bonaventure in 1885, followed by the Observants' College of St. Anthony in 1890 and the Capuchin College of St. Lawrence of Brindisi in 1908. Each of these launched scholarly intellectual journals to promote Franciscan thought.

One of the most successful "prudent adaptations" Franciscans made to cope with the modern world was instituting minor (or "Seraphic") seminaries as means to promote vocations to the Order. As public educational systems began to develop in nineteenth-century Europe, secondary schools were often dominated by a secular, anticlerical philosophy; furthermore, they generally were not accessible to rural youth. And so, the Reformed Franciscans of the Piedmont Province established a Seraphic Seminary for elementary school graduates in 1869, with the aim of providing youth especially from rural areas, where traditional faith practices were still strong, with the specialized religious training required for future clerics. The following year the Capuchins founded one in Tuscany. This innovation—aimed at educating candidates from roughly twelve to eighteen years of age who would then enter novitiate—spread rapidly throughout all three branches of the Order. Their graduates accounted for much of the growth experienced by Franciscans in the late nineteenth and early twentieth centuries.

The major institutional development among the Franciscans during this age of Roman centralization was the reunion of the various families within the Observant branch. Pope Leo XIII, who as a Third Order member was deeply committed to the Franciscan movement, was very concerned about the proliferation of different observances in the same Order, which he viewed as counterproductive and increasingly anachronistic in the light of declining numbers. The pope introduced the topic at the chapter of 1889; after years of sometimes heated internal discussion, Leo finally promulgated the apostolic constitution, *Felicitate Quadam* on October 4, 1897. This decree united all the Observant families, who were henceforth to follow the same general constitutions and wear the same type of habit under one central government. All previous titles—the Regular Observance and the "stricter observant" terms of Reformed, Discalced and Recollect—were abolished. From now on the united friars were to be known simply as "the Order of Friars Minor" (O.F.M.) without any other qualification. Both the Conventuals and the Capuchins, however, were unhappy with Leo's solution, since referring to the former Observant branch simply as Friars Minor seemed to give them a certain priority. As a result, in 1909 Pius X decreed that they also should use a distinction—"O.F.M. of the

Leonine Union"—for official purposes. However, the Order never accepted this terminology and the Vatican itself soon stopped using it.

At the beginning of the new century, Franciscans were making rapid strides in North America. From 1880 to 1920, immigration to the United States had become increasingly diverse as large numbers of Eastern Europeans and Italians poured into the country. Franciscans from those countries quickly followed to meet their spiritual needs. In order to foster vocations from these immigrant communities, distinct units were created within the Conventuals and Friars Minor for friars working in Polish ethnic ministries and within the Friars Minor and Capuchins for those working in Italian ones.

Franciscans were also moving west, returning to lands in which they had ministered during the Spanish mission era. In 1885, the Friars Minor at Mission Santa Barbara, California, were incorporated into the flourishing German-American province of the Sacred Heart, which quickly assumed the care of German ethnic parishes in California cities, as well as work among Native American peoples; a new province, dedicated to Saint Barbara, was erected on the west coast in 1915. The Cincinnati province also initiated an extensive ministry in the southwest among the Navaho and Pueblo peoples beginning in 1898. And English Capuchins also began ministering in California. In Canada, Friars Minor from Montreal began to put down roots in Edmonton, Alberta in 1908.

Franciscans plunged into a wide variety of work with confident enthusiasm in the first half of the twentieth century, both in traditional friar ministries and challenging new efforts. In English-speaking countries, Franciscans tended to assume the care of parishes and schools, besides their traditional ministry of preaching and spiritual direction. Perhaps the breadth of Franciscan presence might best be illustrated through the careers of three notable friars, two of whom have been recognized as saints by the universal church.

Agostino Gemelli (1878–1959) was born into a middle class family in Milan that shared the anticlerical sentiments typical of the era. He studied medicine at the University of Pavia, where he was active in socialist circles. However, shortly after receiving his degree, Gemelli experienced a profound religious conversion and in 1903 entered the Friars Minor. His superiors, recognizing his talents, allowed him to pursue his medical research following his ordination in 1908. The young priest had a number of conversations with the noted philosopher, Cardinal Mercier of Belgium, who inspired Gemelli to enter on his life's work, the reconciliation of faith and modern science through neo-Scholastic philosophy. In 1914, he founded an influential journal of culture, *Vita e Pensiero*. Although drafted into the medical corps of the Italian army in 1915, Gemelli was still able to continue his scientific career, becoming one of the major Italian contributors to experimental psychology.

Gemelli was a ceaseless dynamo of energy. He worked with a prominent laywoman, Armida Barelli, to found the Catholic University of the Sacred Heart in Milan, which opened in 1921 and of which he remained rector until his death. With her, he also initiated a new form of Franciscan consecrated life, the secular institute of the Missionaries of the Kingship of Christ. Gemelli remained active as a scholar, producing the influential work, *The Franciscan Message to the World* (English edition, 1934). In 1937, he was named chair of the Pontifical Academy of Sciences. His long-awaited dream, a major school of medicine in Rome, opened after his death.

His Italian contemporary Padre Pio (1887–1968) had a markedly different background. He was born Francesco Forgione to a devout family in the southern Italian farming village of Pietralcina. Even as a child, he determined to dedicate himself to God. Because of the lack of educational opportunities, his father emigrated to the United States to obtain funds to tutor the young Francesco, who was thus able to enter the Capuchin novitiate in 1903, where he received the name "Pio." The young friar, who had always been plagued with ill health, was assigned in 1916 to the friary in the town of San Giovanni Rotondo in Apulia, where he remained the rest of his life except for a brief stint in the Italian army in World War I.

Pio had always experienced intense spiritual phenomena, but after his release from the military these intensified, culminating in 1918 with the appearance of the stigmata on his body. The wounds bled regularly for the rest of his life. He spent many hours a day hearing confessions, gaining fame for his ability to read the hearts of his penitents. By the 1920s, thousands were flocking to San Giovanni to meet the stigmatic friar. Because of this publicity, Pio fell under intense suspicion from local bishops and the Roman Curia. Gemelli was one of the examiners sent by the Vatican to investigate, concluding that Pio was a self-mutilating psychopath. At one point, he was forbidden to say public Mass and to speak with women. The tide began to turn in the mid 1930s, however, and Padre Pio resumed his life as a confessor. He also founded a modern hospital from contributions raised from devotees, which opened in 1956.

Maximilian Kolbe (1894–1941) was born near Lodz, Poland (then part of the Russian Empire) to a devout but poor family. At the age of thirteen, Kolbe determined to become a Franciscan, and so illegally crossed the border into the Austro-Hungarian Empire where he entered the Conventuals' minor seminary in Lvov. Upon completing his novitiate, he was sent on for studies in Rome, where he earned degrees in both philosophy and theology. During his years in Italy, he witnessed violent anticlerical demonstrations and thus became convinced of the need to mobilize the church against its attackers. While still a student, he organized the Militia of the Immaculate, whose members would consecrate themselves to Mary as the Mediatrix of all graces to work for "the conversion of sinners, heretics, and especially enemies of the Church."

When Kolbe returned to Poland in 1919, he embarked on a whirlwind of activity to advance his Militia. In 1922 he founded a monthly magazine, *Knight of the Immaculate*, which quickly achieved great popularity. To foster this and other projects, he founded the monastery of Niepokalanow ("City of the Immaculate") near Warsaw, which by the late 1930s housed a self-sustaining Franciscan community of almost eight hundred members, putting out a wide variety of publications. When Poland was occupied at the beginning of World War II, the activities of the monastery fell under suspicion by the Nazis. In 1941, Kolbe was arrested by the Gestapo and deported to the concentration camp at Auschwitz. In July, a man from his barracks escaped; in retaliation, the commandant selected ten prisoners to be starved to death. One of these, a young officer, cried out in concern for his wife and children. Kolbe stepped forward to take his place, and so was consigned to the starvation bunker, where he was finally killed by lethal injection.

As the story of Maximilian Kolbe illustrates, despite the generally positive picture for Franciscans in the first half of the century, they did suffer a good deal of persecution, especially with the rise of Communism and other totalitarian governments from the 1920s through the 1950s. When the new Soviet Republic was proclaimed in Russia, Franciscans active in its territory were deported, imprisoned or executed. Violence next came to Spain, where the establishment of a republic in 1931 resulted in numerous anticlerical measures. When a coalition of left-wing parties won the elections in 1936, the country erupted in Civil War. Priests and religious who dwelt in the "Red Zone" were subject to summary execution: Over 220 Friars Minor and 90 Capuchins were butchered. Then, when Germany invaded Poland in 1939, many friars, especially educated ones, were imprisoned or executed. And with the Communist takeover of Eastern Europe and of China after World War II, the ministerial activities of Franciscans in those countries were either totally suppressed or severely curtailed.

Still, by 1960, the Friars Minor had reached 26,300 members; the Capuchins 15,400, and the Conventuals 4,100. A good proportion of them lived in the English-speaking nations of the United States, Canada, Britain, Ireland and Australia: some 5,400 Friars Minor, 1,700 Capuchins and 1,000 Conventuals.

However, the situation was already changing after World War II; as secularization made more inroads in European society, church attendance dropped and vocations began to decline. In response, Pope John XXIII called the Second Vatican Council (1962–1965) to redefine the church's posture to modern society. Influenced by his background as a church historian, John was convinced that the church must adapt its organization and pastoral methods to a fundamentally changed world; for this, he coined the phrase *aggiornamento*—a "bringing up to date" of the church founded on a profound inner renewal. In its final session in 1965, the council issued the decree *Perfectae Caritatis*, which called for the "up-to-date renewal" of the church's religious congregations based on two principles: on the one hand, "a constant return to the sources of Christian life in general and to the primitive inspiration of the institute," and on the other, "their adaptation to the changed conditions of our time."

Following the council, Pope Paul VI issued a *motu proprio, Ecclesiae Sanctae* (1966) to implement this agenda, mandating all religious congregations to hold extraordinary general chapters within three years to revise their constitutions according to the spirit of their founders and the theological principles set forth by the council. Paul recognized that over the years religious congregations may have developed structures and practices which were "alien" to the founder's spirit or "obsolete" in light of modern circumstances; the new constitutions were to eliminate them, and base its legislation firmly on the two principles of reform enunciated in *Perfectae Caritatis*.

All three branches of Friars Minor quickly complied, holding extraordinary general chapters in the late 1960s to draw up new general constitutions. Franciscan prayer life was revised on the basis of the principles enunciated by the council's *Constitution on the Liturgy*, in light of which many traditional devotional and penitential practices were made optional or even eliminated. With regard to the observance of poverty, the Friars Minor and the Capuchins altered two of the features that had traditionally distinguished them from the Conventuals, allowing friars to use money and to accept the "fixed incomes" of government health insurance and old-age pensions since these were generally available to other poor people in modern societies. The principles of collegiality and subsidiarity emphasized in the Constitution on the Church, *Lumen Gentium*, brought about a thoroughgoing revision of government within the three orders. Participation in provincial chapters was made more democratic, and since the decree *Ecclesiae Sanctae* had given relatively broad latitude for communities to draw up new practices on a trial basis (*ad experimentum*), more authority was given for local units to make adaptations to their way of life in light of their particular circumstances. In an attempt to retrieve the early nature of the Lesser Brothers as a true fraternity of equals, all of the Franciscan orders made efforts to incorporate non-ordained brothers in the structures of government and to abolish practices that had grown up over the years that had turned lay friars into second class citizens.

Many of these changes were made in response to the council's call for religious institutes to return to their "primitive inspiration" as a criterion for renewal. Earlier Franciscan reform movements had been dominated by images from the early biographies of Francis produced by friars who were attempting to recount how Francis lived and what he said. This was the first time that primary focus was being given to the writings of Francis himself. New tools of textual criticism allowed Kajetan Esser to produce a critical edition of Francis' writings which became the basis of many vernacular translations. Franciscans began to analyze these writings in light of the context of the thirteenth-century church and make appropriate connections to their own lives. In a very real way, present-day Franciscans are able to attain a better knowledge of their Order's founder than any previous generation except Francis' own Italian contemporaries.

Perhaps most importantly, the council led to a massive revisioning of the mission of the Order. *Lumen Gentium* had emphasized that the ultimate thrust of the church's mission is to proclaim the reign of God. The church was no longer identifying itself with that kingdom; rather, it was to be the herald, sign and servant of a reality larger than itself. The Pastoral Constitution on the Church in the Modern World, *Gaudium et Spes*, emphasized that Christians had to be attentive to "the signs of the times," responsive to the dreams and hopes of people for a more authentic human existence. The world synod of bishops in 1971 followed this up, emphasizing that "action on behalf of justice and participation in the transformation of the world fully appear to us as a constitutive element of the preaching of the Gospel."

Thus, many Franciscans began to perceive their mission as rooted in the church, but reaching beyond its institutional boundaries to work for the transformation of the world. The Friars Minor, for example, proclaimed at their general chapter of 1973:

> The essential mission of our fraternity, its vocation in the Church and in the world, consists of the lived reality of our life-commitment...in the midst of the human community.... We believe therefore that the friars may work at any job or profession that is compatible with the Christian and Franciscan way of life. While it remains necessary to labor...at the service of institutions organized by the Church, we acknowledge the importance of working in the midst of others as a form of service and witness that brings us closer to our fellow human beings.

As that chapter also realized, such a vision, "close to the poor and sensitive to the lot of the oppressed...creates social and political implications." Franciscans, who had always been attentive to works of charity on behalf of the poor, became increasingly involved in working for the transformation of political and economic structures to insure justice for them. Especially in Latin America, many Franciscans became caught up in the movement known as Liberation Theology. The Brazilian Friar Minor Leonardo Boff became one of its foremost spokesmen. In 1985, however, Boff was silenced by the Vatican for a year because of an alleged reliance on Marxist concepts of class warfare in his theology; finally, in light of further criticism, he withdrew from the Order and the priesthood in 1992.

The Boff case vividly illustrates some of the tensions unleashed among Franciscans by the council's call for *aggiornamento*. What exactly was their Order's "primitive inspiration," their distinctive Franciscan "charism"? And how did that charism relate to the larger church? Although on the whole, Franciscans have followed a more "progressive" interpretation of the council's documents, other friars felt that essential values of their religious life were being sacrificed in a rush to accommodate to modern culture, that Franciscan life itself was becoming secularized. As a result of these differing perceptions, as always during times of crisis in the past, new movements have emerged among Franciscans.

Already in 1970, two Conventual friars in Frigento, Italy, Stefano Manelli and Gabriel Pelletieri, stated their desire to renew the Order according to "a Marian Plan for Franciscan life" in the spirit of Maximilian Kolbe. Gaining followers, they finally split from the Conventuals in the late 1980s, forming a new religious institute called the Franciscan Friars of the Immaculate. Due to their considerable spread, Pope John Paul II recognized them as a congregation of pontifical right in 1998. Highly penitential, the friars stress reproducing Jesus' life of "total immolation" through their life of prayer and poverty; they maintain traditional ascetical practices of fasting, silence and the use of the discipline (self-flagellation).

In the United States, eight Capuchin friars, led by the well-known spiritual director Benedict Groeschel, withdrew in 1987 to found a new religious community called the Franciscan Friars of the Renewal. Their aim was "to live the vows of authentic Franciscan life in a way that effectively challenges worldly values, in the spirit of the early Capuchin reform." They were formally established as a diocesan religious institute in 1999. With a commitment to intense communal prayer and a simple style of life, the work of the friars is devoted to hands-on service to the poor and evangelization, especially among youth.

The most significant recent trend in all three branches of the Franciscan Order in the last several decades, however, mirroring developments within the church at large, has been the decline of the Order's membership in Western Europe and North America and its growth in Latin America, Asia and Africa. The patterns of Franciscan expansion to these traditional "mission lands" in the late nineteenth and early twentieth centuries was determined to a great extent by the policies of the Congregation for the Propagation of the Faith: to carve up "mission countries" into Apostolic Vicariates, entrusting each to a specific religious community, which was made responsible for carrying out the work of evangelization in the area. Generally, a member of the congregation was ordained bishop to serve as Vicar Apostolic of the territory. Franciscans, heirs of a great missionary tradition, were assigned a significant number of these vicariates.

For example, in the 1830s, the Holy See contacted the Friars Minor for volunteers as missionaries in China, which was beginning to open up to European contact after a long period of isolation. In 1838, an Italian friar, Giuseppe Rizzolati, was placed in charge of a new vicariate comprising Hubei and Hunan provinces; two new vicariates, Shanxi and Shandong, followed in the next several years. As new vicariates were created, various Franciscan entities continued to respond, so that by the outbreak of World War II, twenty-eight of the church's mission territories in China were staffed by twenty-three different European and North American provinces of the Friars Minor, as well as one native Chinese entity, totaling over 750 friars. Worldwide at that time there were some 2,500 Friars Minor working in territories supervised by the Propagation of the Faith, along with over 1,000 Capuchins and 150 Conventuals.

By the early 1960s, the missionary focus of Franciscans was shifting, striving to implant the Order within the host countries, forming new indigenous units. This move corresponded with the Second Vatican Council's emphasis on local churches' assuming their own unique character. For example, the Franciscan presence in the Philippines had long depended on Discalced missionaries from Spain. In the mid-1890s, prior to the Philippine Revolution and American takeover of the islands, there were some 480 Spanish friars in the country; by 1950 there were only twenty-three. Local bishops began requesting other Franciscan entities to minister in their dioceses. In the course of the decade, the Venetian province and then three U.S. provinces established foundations. Since all of these began to accept native vocations, the various mission units decided to establish a joint formation system for these local candidates, which ultimately led to the erection of a new independent Filipino unit of the Order in 1970.

Perhaps the most meteoric growth of the twentieth century was experienced by the Capuchins in India. With European missionaries active in the northern vicariates of Agra and Lahore, the friars founded a novitiate there in 1922. Since most of the native vocations were southerners, however, the Capuchins decided to transfer it to Farangipet (now in Karnataka state) in 1930. With a promising number of new candidates, the forty friars in India were organized into a general commissariat in 1938. A significant and steady rise in vocations enabled an independent province to be erected in 1963, which has since been divided several times. In addition to their pastoral work, the Capuchins have founded a Franciscan Institute of Spirituality in Bangalore. In 2005, there were over 1,200 Capuchins in India organized in six provinces and several smaller units, making them the most numerous nation in their Order next to the Italians.

Another area of Franciscan resurgence has been Eastern Europe. The Conventual friars, with their historic presence in the region, were poised to take advantage of the revival of religion in the area. In Poland especially, the church was a popular rallying point during the waning decades of Communism. Now, with almost 1,100 friars, the Poles have become the largest nationality among the Conventual friars.

Conclusion

This brief history of the Friars Minor has indicated some of the richness and diversity of the men who have called themselves brothers of Francis of Assisi over the past eight centuries. They have included great thinkers such as Bonaventure, John Duns Scotus and William of Ockham, who made enduring contributions to the Catholic theological tradition. Spiritual writers, such as Francisco de Osuna and Benet of Canfield, have charted the path of union with God. Franciscan missionaries such as John of Montecorvino, Francisco Solano and Junipero Serra blazed the path of Christianity in Asia, the Americas and Africa. Other friars have been deeply committed to serving the poor and the afflicted, organizing countless works of charity; as I complete this book, the Franciscan Order is gaining its latest member to be officially beatified by the church: the Capuchin Yaakub Ghazir Haddad (1875–1954), a popular preacher and founder of several institutions for the chronically ill in his native Lebanon. And, most of all, countless unheralded Franciscans have been known as preachers, confessors, teachers, pastors and workers in the midst of people, loved for their approachability, kindness, self-lessness and lack of pretense.

This wide variety of activities to which Franciscans have devoted themselves indicates that they were not founded to engage in any one particular ministry or corporate apostolate. When Francis looked back at the events of 1208 he stated simply: "After the Lord gave me some brothers, no one showed me what I had to do, but the Most High Himself revealed to me that I should live according to the pattern of the Holy Gospel." For Francis the good news of God's love was revealed in the self-emptying life of the Lord Jesus in whose footsteps he was called to follow. The Rule confirmed by Pope Honorius III in 1223, to which all Franciscan friars commit themselves, states clearly: "The Rule and Life of the Lesser Brothers is this: to observe the Holy Gospel of our Lord Jesus Christ by living in obedience, without anything of one's own, and in chastity."

Contemporary Franciscans have reaffirmed this central gospel vision. A number of years ago, the Friars Minor summed up their role in the contemporary church and world in these words: "We are not an organization structured for one or several specific tasks. We are a community of brothers, who, within the communion of the Church...wish simply to live a Gospel type of life." Like their founder, Franciscans have always emphasized that the gospel must be manifest in life before it is verbalized into a message. The popular saying attributed to Saint Francis captures this conviction: "Preach the gospel always; when necessary, use words."

This gospel type of life for Franciscans has four central components: first, a commitment to be people of prayer, as Francis states in the Rule, "desiring above all else to have the Spirit of the Lord and Its holy activity, to pray to Him always with a pure heart"; second, the commitment to be lesser ones among God's people, "not making anything their own," but, "as pilgrims and strangers in this world," to "serve the Lord in poverty and humility"; third, the commitment to create a brotherhood of mutual "love and care" among themselves, "showing that they are members of the same family"; and fourth, to "go about in the world" as heralds of the peace of God's reign. Other religious congregations have emphasized one or several of these components. Franciscans believe that their evangelical charism demands keeping all four in a creative tension.

We have seen that their sense of mission originally sent Francis and his brothers to work among their neighbors in Assisi, informally spreading the gospel message. But it has also led Franciscans historically to take on a variety of specific ministries on behalf of the church. Thus, even within Francis' lifetime, as the ordained brothers increased in numbers, the Order committed itself especially to the pastoral ministries of doctrinal and moral preaching and the hearing of confessions. That same sense of mission also sent Franciscans out to bring the gospel to other nations, to engage in works of charity among the poor, to become teachers and scholars and to assume the care of parishes.

However, whatever work Franciscans may be involved in, they also have believed that their mission should flow from an authentic brotherhood of prayer, simple living and mutual care. These are the bases of their gospel witness in the world. The Order is a "fraternity-in-mission." It is precisely because Franciscans view these lifestyle issues of prayer, poverty and brotherhood as essential elements of their mission, not peripheral features, that we have seen so many disagreements and even divisions arise among them over the centuries. Often, it was because some friars came to feel that the ministerial structures they had taken on were cramping their spirits that new reform movements have come to birth. The different branches within the Franciscan tradition have come to be known for accentuating one or the other facets of the general charism.

Today, over thirty thousand men belong to Francis' Order of Lesser Brothers in its three major branches—the Friars Minor (often simply called "Franciscans"), the Capuchins and the Conventual Franciscans—making them the largest group of male religious in the Catholic church. They are celebrating their eight-hundredth anniversary at a critical juncture at the beginning of the third

Christian millennium. According to José Rodríguez Carballo, general minister of the Friars Minor, this anniversary cannot simply be about remembering and recounting a glorious history, but a graced moment for the brothers to take up the challenge to "recreate" Francis' charism anew in light of the challenges of the present world: "We wish to return to the essentials of our 'form of life' by rereading it and reincarnating it in the cultural reality of today."

Franciscan friars are fortunate in that their founder, Francis of Assisi, continues to be an inspirational figure for countless people in the world today. But breaking away from the romantic stereotypes and coming to know better the historical Francis also creates some difficulties for Franciscans trying to discern their particular life and mission in the contemporary church. Modern historical research has opened up the gap between the primitive fraternity and the Order as it developed within the first several decades of its existence. So, does going back to the roots of the Franciscan charism mean returning to the life of the early brotherhood (roughly from 1209 to 1220) or, for most of the friars today who are involved in ecclesial ministry, does it mean reclaiming the values of the Lesser Brothers as they began committing themselves to advance the pastoral mission of the church (1220–1250)? Perhaps some might even come to the conclusion that the personal charism of Francis is one thing, and the charism of the Order of Friars Minor another.

Franciscans will continue to wrestle with their founder's legacy and their subsequent history. The important thing is that they allow Francis' powerful reading of the gospel of Jesus Christ to shape their lives. If they do so, then the Order of Lesser Brothers will continue to bring Francis' message of "peace and good" to the church and the entire world for years to come.

Annotated Bibliography
(confined to English-language studies)

The only detailed general history of the entire course of Franciscan history available in English is Lazaro Iriarte, O.F.M., CAP., *Franciscan History: The Three Orders of St. Francis of Assisi*, trans. Patricia Ross (Chicago: Franciscan Herald, 1982). There are also the more popular treatments of William Short, *The Franciscans* (Collegeville, Minn.: Liturgical, 1989), and Damien Vorreux and Aaron Pembleton, *A Short History of the Franciscan Family* (Chicago: Franciscan Herald, 1989).

There are several important studies of the Franciscan Order in the Middle Ages (down to 1517). The most thorough and comprehensive study remains: John Moorman, *A History of the Franciscan Order, from its Origins to the Year 1517* (Chicago: Franciscan Herald, 1998).

Many of the early sources for Franciscan history, both the writings of Francis himself and the early biographies, as well as related documents from the period, are now available in *Francis of Assisi: Early Documents*, Regis Armstrong, O.F.M. CAP., Wayne Hellmann, O.F.M. CONV., and William Short, O.F.M., eds.:

Volume 1: *The Saint* (New York: New City, 1999).

Volume 2: *The Founder* (New York: New City, 2000).

Volume 3: *The Prophet* (New York: New City, 2001).

Volume 4: *Index* (New York: New City, 2002).

Other important studies on the Franciscans in the Middle Ages are:

Brooke, Rosalind. *Early Franciscan Government* (Cambridge: Cambridge University Press, 1959).

Burr, David. *The Spiritual Franciscans: From Protest to Persecution in the Century after St. Francis* (Philadelphia: Pennsylvania State University Press, 2001).

Fleming, John W. *An Introduction to the Franciscan Literature of the Middle Ages* (Chicago: Franciscan Herald, 1977).

Flood, David. *Francis of Assisi and the Franciscan Movement* (Quezon City, Philippines, 1989).

Manselli, Raoul. *St. Francis of Assisi.* Paul Duggan, trans. (Chicago: Franciscan Herald, 1988)

Merlo, Grado G. *In the Name of Francis*, English translation of *Nel Nome di San Francesco* (St. Bonaventure, N.Y.: Franciscan Institute, 2008).

Nimmo, Duncan. *Reform and Division in the Franciscan Order, from Saint Francis to the Foundation of the Capuchins* (Rome: Capuchin Historical Institute, 1987).

Robson, Michael. *The Franciscans in the Middle Ages* (Woodbridge: Boydell, 2006).

The modern history of the Franciscans has not fared as well in English-language scholarship. Although a number of books and articles have treated specific aspects of that history, more general works are few. Recommended are:

Carmody, Maurice. *The Leonine Union of the Order of Friars Minor* (St. Bonaventure, N.Y.: Franciscan Institute, 1994).

Cuthbert [Hess], Father, o.s.f.c. *The Capuchins: A Contribution to the History of the Counter-Reformation* (New York: Longmans, Green, and Company, 1929).

Morales, Francisco, O.F.M., ed. *Franciscan Presence in the Americas: Essays on the Activities of the Franciscan Friars in the Americas, 1492-1900* (Potomac, Md.: Academy of American Franciscan History, 1983).

Phelan, John Leddy. *The Millennial Kingdom of the Franciscans in the New World* (Los Angeles: University of California Press, 1970).

Index

resistance against John XXIII, 72
restrictions on, during
Enlightenment, 120–122
tension with secular clergy, 56
See also brotherhood, Capuchins,
Discalced Franciscans, friars,
Friars Minor, Lesser Brothers,
Minorite movement, Observants,
Order, Recollect Franciscans,
Reformed Friars Minor
fraticelli, 78–79
fratres minores, naming selves, 22
Frederick I Barbaarossa, 4
French Observants, 81–82
French Recollects, 100
French Revolution, and exclaustration of
friars, 122–123
frescoes, 65–66
friars
cloistering of, 75
exclaustrated, 122–123, 125
expelled from theology faculty, 56
overpopulation of, 120
stereotypes, 77
tortured in Netherlands and France,
101
Friars Minor, 91
contemporary, 153
numbers in twentieth century, 143
proclamation of 1973, 145–146
Reformed, 99–100

Gante, Pedro de, 108–109
Gemelli, Agostino, 140
*General History of the Things of New
Spain*, 110
general minister, limiting power of, 53
Geoffroi, Raymond, 68–69
Geoghegan, Bonaventure, 129
Gerard of Modena, 48–49
Gerardo of Borgo San Donnino, 56–58
German-Belgian Recollects, 100
Germany, friars banished from houses
in, 94
Giles (brother), 18

Gospel of Christ, passages reinforcing
brotherhood, 18
"Gospel type of life," four components
of, 152–153
governments, liberal, and suppression of
religious orders, 124–125
Great Devotion, 48
"Great Pact" of 1210, 19
Great Western Schism, 81–82
Gregory IX
efforts to reform Christian society, 42
endorsement and support of Lesser
Brothers, 48–49
See also Ugolino (cardinal)
Gregory VII, 4
Guadalupe, Juan de, 89–90
Guido (bishop), support of, 17

Haddad, Yaakub Ghazir, 151
Haymo of Faversham, 49, 52–53
Hennepin, Louis, 112
Henry VIII, break with Rome, 94–95
heretical sects, 7–8, 37
hierarchy, within Order, development of,
76
History of the Indian Church, 110
History of the Mongols, 63
History of New Spain, 110
Holy Land, friars' establishment in, 74
Honorius III, and evangelical move-
ments, 34

Iberian peninsula
as chief agent of Franciscan
expansion, 105
See also Spain
Inca empire, conquest of, 110
India
conversions in, 113–114
meteoric growth of Capuchins in,
148–149
Innocent IV, 54–55, 57
Innocent III, 10, 21–22
Ireland
establishing province in, 47
Observants flourishing in, 103

missions
  to China, 62–64
  early, 27–28
  to eastern and northern Europe,
    46–47
  to England, 46–47
  to Germany, 45–46
  from Iberian peninsula, 105–111
  as means of religious revival, 97
  to Muslim countries, 29, 36, 41
  North American, 108–112, 129–133,
    139
  South American, 110–112
Moirans, Epifanio, 113
Morocco, expeditions to, 29, 36
Murner, Thomas, 93
Muslims, Francis and, 28–30
Musso, Cornelio, 96
mysticism, 97

Nagasaki, twenty-six martyrs of, 115
natives, reception to Christianity, 107
Netherlands, friars martyred in, 101
New Mexico, Franciscans established in,
  111
New World, conquistadores in, 107–108
Nicholas III, 67
Nicholas IV, 61–66
North America
  Capuchins in, 112
  Franciscan expansion in U.S.,
    129–133, 139
  Franciscans' arrival in Florida, 111
  Franciscans' decline in, 147
  missions in Canada, 112, 126
  reestablishing missions in American
    West, 139
  See also California missions, Mexico
novices
  attempts to limit numbers, 120, 122
  and temporary vows, 125
novitiate, establishing year of, 35

Observants, 80–86
  all-time high in numbers, 119–120
  flourishing in Ireland, 103

Irish, 127–128
  reestablished in France, 126
  reunion of various families, 138–139
  sent on missions to Mexico, 108
  vs. Conventuals, 85–88
Ochino, Bernardino, 95
O'Donnell, James, 128
Odoric of Pordenone, 64
O'Farrell, Peter, 129
Olivi, Peter John, 68–69
Order
  "divorce" within, 88
  papal investigation of, 70
  reform efforts within. See
    reformation, efforts toward
  revisioning of mission, 145–146
  Second and Third, 39–40, 65
  segments within, , 85, 87–88,
    146–147. See also Capuchins,
    Discalced Franciscans, Friars
    Minor, Observants vs. Conventuals,
    Recollect Franciscans
Order of Preachers, 32, 34
Order of Saint Clare, origins of, 39–40
Ot, Guiral, 78–79

Paoluccio. See Vagnozzi, Paolo
papacy
  first Franciscan named to, 61
  marginalization of, 121
  See also individual popes
Paravas, conversions among, 114
Parenti, John, 41, 45
Pascual, Juan, 89–90
paternalism, in missionaries' work in
  Mexico, 109
Paul VI, 143
Pecham, John, 73
Pelikan, Konrad, 93–94
penance
  embarking on life of, 11
  preaching, 20–21
  reestablishment of, 125
  See also Brothers and Sisters of
    Penance
Perfectae Caritatis, 143